Published by:
Yore Publications
12 The Furrows, Harefield,
Middx. UB9 6AT.

© Mike George 1995

....

British Library Cataloguing-in-Publication Data.
A catalogue record for this book
is available from the British Library.

ISBN 1 874427 46 1

(Every effort has been made to acknowledge the source of illustrations
and to ensure that copyright has not been infringed)

YORE PUBLICATIONS specialise in football books, generally of an historical nature, including Club Histories, Who's Who Books, and general interest - both League and non-League. Three free newsletters per year are issued. For your first newsletter please send a S.A.E. to the above address.

Printed by The Book Factory

INTRODUCTION

GETTING TO KNOW THE STONES

So how did a Londoner first get attracted to a team like Maidstone United? It's a long story, and not as interesting as it might be, however in the interests of validity, I present an abbreviated version.

As a child, my earliest memories were of living in Downham, between Bromley and Catford. We then moved to Orpington in Kent. It was here that my love of football developed and grew, although perhaps because my father claimed allegiance to Aston Villa - insisting at every opportunity that they were the greatest Club in Britain - and Orpington being full of a mixture of Arsenal, Chelsea, Charlton and Millwall fans (and a few of Crystal Palace), I never really followed one Club.

The first match I ever saw was at the, 'Den', home of Millwall Football Club, who predictably were playing Aston Villa. My Father had got seat tickets and had taken my brother and myself along, presumably in an attempt to 'convert' us to the claret and blue cause. I don't remember too much about the game, except the Millwall fans urging someone called Derek Posse, to, *"skin 'em"*, and for Harry Cripps to *"get stuck in"* - something, I later learned, he was rather good at. For Aston Villa, I remember Andy Lochead rose above a stationary Millwall defence to head a powerful goal, but couldn't understand why this required the Millwall fans to throw bricks and bottles at the Directors box. Whatever the reason, I vowed to return to 'The Den' to find out!

I did indeed begin to follow the 'Lions' of Millwall, but also attended matches at a variety of other South London grounds. I was privileged to watch the great 1970's Chelsea side, with players such as Osgood, Hudson, Hutchinson, Baldwin, MacCreadie, and my favourite boyhood hero, Charlie 'The wizard' Cooke. I also watched Charlton Athletic, with Peacock, Flannagan and Shipperley - a literal giant in defence (he was about 6'-4"). A little later Crystal Palace enjoyed the dubious benefit of my attendance, but not regularly. My Grandmother lived in Lancing, Sussex, therefore when I stayed there I would trot along to the Goldstone and watch Brighton, then a perennial third division team. They boasted a goalkeeper with the intriguing name of Geoff Sidebottom.......I was certainly intrigued enough to watch them when I could.

It was during this period that I was invited to watch Maidstone United play Exeter City in the F.A. Cup. Under duress, I was seduced to travel Kent to watch the Stones produce an unexpected 1-0 victory, I was however not impressed enough to consider making regular trips. Fate however played a hand, and drew the Stones to play Charlton Athletic at the Valley. The non-League team played well, securing a replay after a fighting 1-1 draw, and it was then back to Maidstone to see the replay. Charlton won, but only after Maidstone had performed well enough to scare the League side. The London Road stadium also recorded a record crowd of around 10,000, and a floodlight failure that day!

It was not until 1980 that I saw the Stones again, this time playing at Gillingham in an F.A. Cup replay that had already produced two draws. Not having seen the first two matches, I was surprised by the size of the Stones support, and also by the intensity of their dislike of the Gills. This was on a par with the hatred of West Ham that Millwall fans harboured. The delight then was infectious, as the League side was beaten by a Maidstone team that were frankly better than the Gills, who were at the time high up in Division 3. One of their defenders scored the first, then the second - a Frank Ovard goal - was a cheeky and totally outrageous lob, which had everyone gasping......the Gills had been beaten by their non-League rivals and would never be allowed to forget it!

About this time, I joined the Army, and was posted abroad to Germany. My football viewing was therefore confined to watching German club sides, a worthy substitute. I visited Hannover 96, Hamburg SV, Bayern Munich (Vs. Aberdeen in the European Cup), Eintract Frankfurt, Schalke 04 - the German equivalent (in terms of notrious fans) of Millwall - and my personal favourites, VFB Stuttgart, who included a young and very skilful, Jurgen Klinnsman. I served in Germany for 5 years, during which time my parents had moved to Maidstone, thus everytime I returned home on leave, I would check the local papers to see whether Maidstone United were at home. On a few of occasions I travelled to away matches as the allegiance grew - to Kettering, Telford, Gateshead, and to two matches in a marathon F.A. Cup tie at Southwick. I watched and celebrated as Maidstone won the Alliance Premier League, and by then was a confirmed Stones fan.

I still had a soft spot for Millwall, but hated the tedious train journey, thus saw them only rarely. When I left the Army in 1986, I returned to Germany to work, leaving Maidstone United to solve their own problems under the guidance of Barry Fry, who was sacked later in the season. I stayed in Europe for 3 years, and returned to England at the end of the 1988-89 season, having learned that Maidstone United had won the GM Vauxhall Conference, and thus promotion to the Football League. Obviously there were other reasons for returning, but Maidstone's promotion certainly had some influence. I vowed to watch them at home and away during this historic season. I nearly achieved a 100% record, missing just two matches, but what I did see was more than worth it. Thus, was I introduced to Maidstone United, and became one of their most fervent supporters. Periods living in Devon and Folkestone followed, but returns to Maidstone were managed, to watch the Stones, at least once or twice a month, and sometimes more.

I first got the idea of this book after the success of the first season in the Football League. However I didn't start writing until a couple of years later, and although it began out as a simple celebration of that first ever Football League season, it has finished up as a brief history, via many changes of direction and rewrites in betweeen! I am sure that I have not missed out items of importance, but there are others around who can fill in any missing gaps. For all that, I hope that you, the reader, enjoy it anyway.

At this point, I must thank those people who have helped me on the project. Alan Brigden, who was always the official Club historian, and I am sure that this work will not be a threat to his status, helped me out with a myriad of useful and interesting material. To Leigh Edwards who provided some useful and valuable last minute information. Thanks must also go to Mike Evans, the Stone's Programme Editor and Alan Goodrich, who provided many of the photos., also of course to Keith Slater, the 'man with the Nikon' for permission to use them.

Others who have helped out included Mark Bristow, and the Kent Messenger Group, for permission to use extracts from match reports and aticles, but most of all, to the players, fans and board of Maidstone United Football Club. Without them, there would have been nothing to write about, and no memories for me to hold. I would also like to thank Dave Twydell of Yore publications for having the foresight, and indeed faith to publish a book about a club with a comparatively small support, even at their height. I hope that those supporters who do remember the Stones fondly, will purchase a copy and make all our efforts worthwhile.

Lastly, and certainly not least, I must give thanks to my wife, Sue, for endless cups of tea, coffee and patience over the three or so years whilst I wrote, rewrote and lost my temper over this work.

M.George

Mike George

Born in London, Mike's first football was watched at a variety of London grounds, including Chelsea, Millwall Crystal Palace and Fulham.

In 1980, he joined the Army, originally for 3 years, however, eventually 7 years were served. The family home had, during this time, moved to Maidstone, and Mike naturally went to watch maidstone United. On leaving the Army, Mike returned to West Germany, where he had served, and became a freelance broadcaster for the British Forces Broadcasting Service, but maintained a keen interest in the Stones.

He returned to the U.K. in 1990, and worked for *RTM Radio* in South London, before moving to *Devonair* in Exeter. He soon moved on to work in the Commercial Department at Elmore A.F.C. in Tiverton, before returning to the South-east, where he took up the post of Commercial Manager for Hythe Town F.C. During this period trips to Maidstone were made as frequent as possible in order to watch the Stones. For a while Mike worked in the club shop at Watling Street, and produced 'Yellow Fever', and 'Golden Days', two Maidstone United fanzines. Shortly after the demise of the Stones, work began on this history, which has taken nearly 4 years to compile.

Mike now regularly watches Millwall and runs a local club, Maidstone Athletic F.C., who play in the Maidstone and District League, with the hope that they may progress to more senior football.

I would like to dedicate this work to all Maidstone United fans - who only have dreams of what might have been.

FOREWORD

I was delighted to be asked to pen the foreword to this book, although at the same time, saddened by events of the most recent past.

I watched from afar, first with elation, and then dismay, as the 'Stones' achieved League status, only to crash back again. What should have been the start of a new, exciting, era for the Club, was not to be.

As a schoolboy, growing up in Yalding, my first heroes were not stars from the Football League, they were people like Jimmy Fletcher, Danny Wiltshire, Denis Cutbush and Fred Baker, all great players and servants of Maidstone United. I have great memories of great football characters such as Arthur Clarke (Chairman), Dick Pritchard (Secretary) and Pete Goddard (Trainer), all of whom taught me lessons that stood me in good stead for my career in the great game.

Despite living 'Up North' in Manchester for more than 30 years, my affection for the town remains intact, and I just hope that somehow, somewhere, there are enough people who care, so that maybe there can be a future, not just a past, for Maidstone United.

David Sadler

CONTENTS

YORE PUBLICATIONS

YORE PUBLICATIONS have become one of the leading publishers specialising in football books, which are generally of an historic nature. Our titles include club histories (Kilmarnock, Newport County, Notts.County, Rotherham United, etc.), non-League (including the 'Gone But Not Forgotten' series - defunct clubs and grounds), General interest (including the much acclaimed 'Rejected F.C.' books - histories of the ex-Football League clubs), 'Who's Whos' (e.g. Lincoln City, Coventry City, Mansfield Town, etc.). Three free newsletters are issued per year, which provide the full details of our titles. Please send a S.A.E. for your first copy to:

Yore Publications, 12 The Furrows, Harefield, Middx. UB9 6AT

CHAPTER 1

HESITANT BEGINNINGS

The Athletics Ground at the turn of the century, note the old pavilion and racing track.

The Maidstone United story, certainly to begin with, was inextricably intertwined with the history of the Athletic Ground, on the A20/London Road in Maidstone.

In the 1880's, the Bath and West show had been held on the ground, which had previously been a hop garden and orchard. In 1893, a group of businessmen decided that it was the ideal place to lay down foundations for a sports arena where cycling, cricket and athletics events could be staged. A football and cricket pitch were laid out with a cinder track for cycling.

Initially, seats for 500 spectators were also installed. The first ground secretary was J.S.Welch, who was succeeded in 1896 by C.S. Craven, who had been one of the founders of Darlington F.C. in 1883. He would go on to hold the position for the next fifty years. Maidstone United were officially formed in 1891, and named Maidstone Invicta. They played their first match at nearby Peneden Heath and within a year had joined the newly formed Maidstone and District League. At this time they played in yellow and black stripes and were nicknamed, "The Canaries". By 1895, having joined Division 2 of the Kent League, they could be found playing at Solomon's Field, Vinters Park, however in 1896 they moved to Postley Fields, Tovil, near Maidstone, joined the Kent League Division 1, and turned Professional.

At this time, the Athletic Ground was used by an amateur team by the name of "Mid Kent", but unfortunately they were not highly successful and suffered a plethora of heavy defeats. The side was disbanded, which meant a financial strain for the ground, which had been losing money.

In June 1897, at the annual meeting of the Maidstone Invicta committee, it was proposed that the Club should change it's name to Maidstone United. Thus on Saturday, August 28 1897, the Chairman, Edmund Vaughan, accompanied by J.S. Welch visited the offices of The Football Association, which at that time were in Chancery Lane, and following discussion with F.J. Wall, the Secretary of the F.A., the name was officially changed.

The 'new' club played it's first ever match at Postley fields against St Stephens, a team from London in front of a crowd of 500. The Maidstone Club won 15-0, a record score that would never be beaten.

Although this sounds very impressive, there was a typhoid scare in Kent at the time, and many teams refused to come and play, which may have been one reason for the high goal tally!

On April 20th 1898, a new committee at the Athletic Ground, decided to take on a lease at a cost of £165 per year. To mark the occasion, Maidstone United

London Road spectators - around 1900

were invited to play Chatham Town in a friendly match. United were beaten 4-1, however the occasion is noteworthy for the fact that Jimmy Sandford became the first Maidstone United player ever to score on the ground. So impressed were Maidstone United with the venue, (and unimpressed with the fact that they would have to pay an increased rent at Postley fields), they arranged to move to the Athletic Ground on a full time basis, playing their first ever competitive match against Swanscombe on September 10th 1898. The Club won 4-0 in front of around 650 spectators. That inaugural season saw Maidstone United win the Kent League Championship, the East Kent League and the Kent Senior Cup.

Maidstone United had announced their arrival in emphatic fashion, and over the next 93 years, they were to rise from a mediocre non-League side, to Professional Football League promotion candidates. Their history would be littered with financial problems and controversy. But in 1898, no one could have envisaged such a future, everything was rosy and bright, the team had begun well, attracted a healthy crowd and actually had a small profit in the bank.

Around the turn of the century, Maidstone United boasted a couple of internationals. One, Tommy Chapman, a Welsh International who had previously played for Manchester City, appeared more than 200 times for the club before retiring in 1907. In April 1902, Tommy Thompson set a personal record scoring 7 goals in an 11-0 victory over his previous club, Dartford. The other was a player recorded only as 'A. Newman', it later cmerged that he was none other than Kent Cricketer, Wally Hardinge, who went on to open for England against Australia with the famous Jack Hobbs in 1921. As a player for Maidstone United he scored over 30 goals. The following year he scored 40 in 41 games! In 1905, he signed for Newcastle United, who to cement the deal, bought their famous team to play the Stones, in 1907. The Magpies won 5-2 in front of an impressive crowd of over 5,000 spectators.

In 1906, the club introduced turnstiles at the ground, three for an entrance charge of 6d (2½p), and one at 3d for ladies, boys and servicemen in uniform. Previously tickets had been available outside the ground, but were no longer on sale, however season tickets could be bought. With the Club in some financial difficulty, they must have been more than pleased with the £100 gate receipts from the Newcastle United match. But very often, loyal fans and officials found that they were called upon to help the club out. One such person was a local draper, Tommy Armstrong. He often stepped in with cash when the club needed it and became Chairman of the club from 1913-1920. He was connected with the club for over 60 years, and is honoured to this day by having a road in Maidstone named after him.

Following Tommy Armstrong as Chairman, came Capt Herbert Sharp. He was a member of the town's confectionery making family, and was born in Week Street, Maidstone, in 1879, the son of Sir Edward Sharp, who was noted for his confectionery. Herbert served in both the Boer and the Great War with some distinction.

Herbert Sharp

Captain Sharp was known for his shrewdness, a characteristic which became apparent both in his dealings with Maidstone United and his business. For instance, having heard that Scottish International, Jimmy McMullen was unhappy with Partick Thistle, he made the long Journey north and arranged an audacious deal for the player to come and play for Maidstone United.

It might appear strange that a professional player of such standing would even consider a move to a club like Maidstone,

Jimmy McMullen

however, Captain Sharp was obviously a clever and persuasive man. The first thing that McMullen said, on hearing the proposal was, *"Where's Maidstone?"* Despite this comment, McMullen signed, and was to become an integral part of the most successful Maidstone side ever. They won the Kent Senior Cup in 1920 when they beat Gravesend in front of a huge crowd of 11,000 fans, enjoyed a good F.A.Cup run which ended in defeat by local rivals, Gillingham, and finished runners-up to Charlton Athletic in the Kent League.

The following season surpassed even this. The Club won the Kent League by 10 points, and added the Thames-Medway Championship, The Kent Senior Cup, Kent Senior Shield and Chatham Charity Cup! In 1922, the Club took more Scotsmen on, as an influx of workers arrived to work at the Kreemy Toffee works in St Peters Street in Maidstone. That year the Club won the Kent Senior Cup, beating Sittingbourne 3-2 in front of nearly 13,000 people.

Despite the on-field successes, Captain Sharp had invested heavily in the Club, and he felt that the returns on his financial outlay were insufficient to justify continuing. Therefore, in 1923, he announced that he was to step down as Chairman. Jimmy Welch, who had been a founder member of the Club, took over and the Kent League was won again.

In 1925, Jimmy McMullen returned to Partick Thistle and went on to attain great success for both Club and Country, which included his part in the 5-1 thrashing of England at Wembley in 1928, where he was captain. The Scots so devastated England, that his team were known as 'The Wembley Wizards'. Jimmy McMullen later returned to Sharps' factory several times to give talks. He didn't, however, have any trouble locating Maidstone!

In May 1926, the Club announced that it was in serious financial trouble, to the extent that the following season the team was made up mostly amateur players, who played in a largely professional League. The years up to the Second World War became a period in the doldrums for the club, as they suffered heavy defeats on a regular basis. When war broke out, the Club was put into mothballs as it had been during the Great War. It was to be 1946 when the Club eventually resumed activity, but not until the late 1980's was it able to emulate anything like the success of the 1920's.

The victorious team of 1921/22. Major trophies won that season:
Thames & Medway Combination, Kent Senior Cup, Chatham Charity Cup,
Kent League Champions Shield, Gilbert Parker Shield.

The period after the war continued as one of disappointment for the Stones. Since 1926, they had not won anything, and were becoming the perennial 'journeymen' of Kentish Football. The club was using amateur players and had not only a lack of success but also of crowds. During the early 1920's, the stadium had regularly seen gates of 2,000, but during the early 1950's they struggled to record hundreds, reflecting the form of the team. Two appearances in the Kent Amateur Cup Final, both as losers, failed to excite the club's fans in Maidstone, and it was not until 1953/54 that the team repeated that feat, when they again lost.

The following year the reserves finished runners-up in the Corinthian League's Neale Cup, a success which spurred the first team on to win the Corinthian League Memorial Shield, The Corinthian League, and the Kent Amateur Cup - all in the next season! However, the team's form was inconsistent, since they reached the Kent Amateur Cup Final the following year, but again lost. In 1957/58, the team finished as runners-up in the Athenian League, and that, as far as Maidstone United were concerned, was that.

The 1950's had been disappointing, although a charitable view might suggest that the Club was in a (long!) period of consolidation, and there had been a few memorable events. Most older fans recall the player Jimmy Fletcher, a striker who signed from local Kent rivals, Faversham. On his debut, he scored four goals in under half an hour against unfortunate Uxbridge! By the end of the 1955/56 season he scored 36 goals in 44 games, which helped the club to the Corinthian League Championship and their two cup successes. Jimmy became the first active Maidstone player to win International recognition, when he was picked to play for the England amateur team against Wales in 1956. He went on to win 4 caps in total whilst with Maidstone.

Corinthian League Champions 1955/56. (players only)
(Back): Baker, Reynolds, D.Fillery, R.Fillery, Harris.
(Front): Cutbush, Fletcher, Wiltshire, Wallis, James, Burnett.

The 1960's were to see an improvement for United, as they opted to join the Isthmian League from the Athenian League in which they had been playing. They found that the Isthmian was much harder, but the appointment of ex-Gillingham forward, Hughie Russell, as coach, improved the team's performances markedly. In 1960/61, a young lad named David Sadler, a graduate from a local school, made his debut aged 15. He went on to score 37 goals in 50 matches before signing for Manchester United. Sadler, probably the most famous player ever to have played for the Stones, went on to fame and fortune with the 'Red Devils'

Championship winning side, played in the infamous European Cup victory over Benfica in 1968, and won International caps at youth, amateur and full international level.

After Sadler's departure in 1963, Maidstone's form once more dipped, with a succession of Managers and players coming and going. There were however some trophies won during the 1960's, the Kent Amateur Cup was won twice, in 1961 and 1962, The Bromley Hospital Cup was added in 1962, and the Kent Senior Cup was captured in 1966. But these in reality, were minor trophies compared to what was on offer. During the 1960's, the worst time for the club was between 1966-1968, and only 10 points were won in one season, when the final goal difference read: for - 59, against - 221.

On the whole the 1960's were an improvement on the previous decade, but it was clear to almost everyone that something had to change. The ground was barely adequate, very much of a non-League enclosure, and not particularly impressive. The Stone's results were indifferent and the local inhabitants not bothered. The Club was stagnant, with little idea of where it was going, or indeed, how to get there. It appeared that the board of Directors were happy to see the club jogging along, with no particular place to go. It needed someone to take over and sort it out before the Club withered and died. That someone was to become the bastion on which the club 'rebuilt' itself. He would, in time, prove to be controversial, but dynamic, with clear ideas of where he wanted to take the club. He was a young, energetic and entrepreneurial businessman by the name of Jim Thompson.

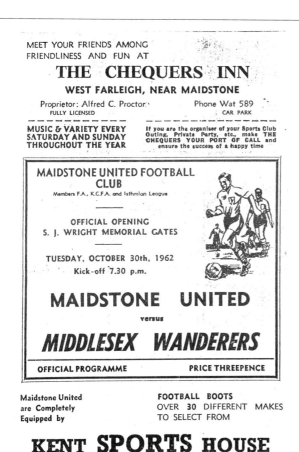

(Left) The Stones team included a very young David Sadler, who went on to fame with Manchester United.

(Below) Three new players for the 1964/65 season: Manager Harry Hill welcomes Peter Busby, Dave Brown and Ken Fulkes.

CHAPTER 4

THE WHIRLWIND ARRIVES

It was November 1970, when Jim Thompson - then 37 years of age was appointed Chairman of Maidstone United. The previous Chairman, Vic Hole, resigned. Jim Thompson's reign at the club was to last until their demise, and throughout, this period was littered with controversy.

During that first November he immediately became an influential figure, having a hand in the splitting of the Southern League into Northern and Southern sections. Stones first match in the Southern section began ignominiously, when they lost 3-1 at Canterbury City. Despite this set-back, Jim Thompson declared that the club was beginning it's quest for Football League status, a brash statement given their standing at that time.

It was to be a long and rocky road, that in retrospect - certainly at first - saw Jim Thompson assume the same kind of status as the famous ravens at the Tower of London. It seemed whatever happened, as long as Jim Thompson was there, the Stones would never fall. Such was the belief that he inspired into the staff and supporters of the club, he was even known affectionately as 'Uncle Jim'. But, in the end, nearly all of the supporters and staff had turned against him, seriously doubting the rhetoric, which began to repeat itself more and more often. It was, apparently, always someone else's fault, and Jim often criticised the Council and local media as being unimaginative and small minded. When the end finally came, many blamed only Jim Thompson, although, on the face of it, the Club's poor finances were at fault.

But, whilst Jim Thompson insists that he never made a financial killing from being Chairman of Maidstone United, he certainly did make many enemies, a fact that had just as much to do with the collapse of the Stones as the debts. Almost everyone agrees that Jim Thompson created an empire, an empire of which he was the Emperor. As so often with 'emperors', there is a very thin line between success - and thus support from one's supporters - and abject failure with seemingly everything and everyone turning gainst you. Like a love affair, the first thrill of a new relationship, especially one that intense, can end up leaving a sour and very bitter taste.

When Jim Thompson took over the club though, it was languishing near the bottom of the Isthmian League, attendances were between 100 and 200 and there was a woeful lack of organisation. Jim Thompson was undaunted, and set about reorganising the club with a vengeance. In May 1972, Bobby Houghton became the first of many managerial casualties, when he was sacked, and Ernie Morgan replaced him.

Southern League Champions 1972/73: (Back): Prichard, May, Tough, Sheridan, Barker, Dunbar, Maggs, Walker, Richardson, Lillis, Basey, Stepney, Drury. (Front): Watson, Kalinka, Oliver, Morgan, Angel, Thompson, McVeigh, Evans.

The first honours came exactly a year later as Maidstone United were crowned Southern League, First Division South Champions, whereupon they were promoted to the Premier Division. In 1973/74, they won the Kent Messenger Trophy and were Finalist in the Kent Senior Cup, beaten by Margate. The following season they reached the Final again, beaten this time by Tonbridge, but the following year they won it, lifting the trophy for the first time since 1966.

In 1976 the first ground improvements were begun - car park, stands, the pitch, and terracing. Over the years, nothing was overlooked as Jim Thompson realised that without a decent ground, the dream of Football League status was hopeless. In addition to football, the Chairman introduced Greyhound racing, and later Rugby League to the stadium, he wanted to create a 'sporting' atmosphere for all the family.

On December 16th 1978, Maidstone faced Exeter City at the Athletic Ground, (by now unofficially renamed, "Maidstone stadium"), in the F.A. Cup. Over 3,000 watched as the Stones became 'Giantkillers' for the first time, although perhaps because they beat the Professionals by just a solitary goal there was barely any publicity other than from the local media.

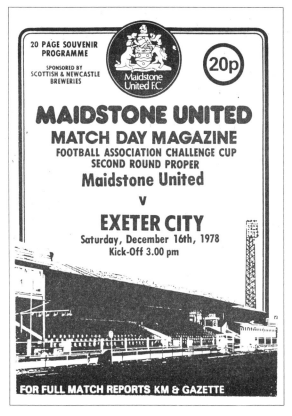

20 PAGE SOUVENIR PROGRAMME

SPONSORED BY SCOTTISH & NEWCASTLE BREWERIES

Maidstone United F.C.

20p

MAIDSTONE UNITED

MATCH DAY MAGAZINE

FOOTBALL ASSOCIATION CHALLENGE CUP
SECOND ROUND PROPER

Maidstone United

v

EXETER CITY

Saturday, December 16th, 1978
Kick-Off 3.00 pm

FOR FULL MATCH REPORTS KM & GAZETTE

It certainly wasn't recognised as a mighty scalp to be recalled on countless occasions by the BBC, whenever discussing the feats of 'non-League giantkilling'. Perhaps if it had been another club - Yeovil Town, for instance who have an enviable 'reputation' for 'Giantkilling' the feat may have been recalled. Gillingham had always been known as 'a football outpost', therefore Maidstone, just a few miles nearer London, were apparently tarred with the same brush. Jim Thompson saw this as one of his tasks in life, to change the image of not only the Club, but perhaps even the town, and to a great extent he did just that.

In the next round, Maidstone travelled to Charlton's famous Valley stadium, and in front of almost 14,000 forced the 'Valients' to a replay after a Glenn Coupland goal had made sure of a 1-1 draw. Back at London Road, attendance records were broken as 10,700 piled in to cheer the Stones on. Maidstone surprised their League visitors with their skill and tenacity. The non-Leaguers did score, but that and an 88th minute floodlight failure failed to stop Charlton netting twice to go through to the 4th round. Whilst Jim Thompson realised that his team had no chance of getting anywhere near Wembley in the competition, he realised that such results would get them noticed. On the basis that any publicity is good publicity, Jim Thompson was to ensure that Maidstone got plenty.

The 1970's were really the foundation upon which the 'dream' was built. The Chairman realised that the amateur status had to go, to be replaced not only by his players being semi-professional, but also by having total commitment and a professional attitude. Managers, players and staff came and went, mostly in a search for those with not only the ability but the dedication which Jim Thompson wanted.

Although he denies that he had any involvement with the playing staff, there are certainly stories from deposed Managers complaining of 'interference', and it is certainly true that the Chairman's influence spread to all parts of the Club. A better calibre of player was attracted to Maidstone United, and whilst it would be nice to imagine that it was Jim's persuasiveness that bought them to Kent, it is probably more realistic to believe the stories of huge wages. Professionalism became a watchword at Maidstone United, and just as many visitors to the club praised the top class administration and organised welcome that they received, as those who complained.

To say that Jim Thompson was impervious to criticism is not strictly true, however he might answer, with perhaps some justification perhaps, that these people all had a grudge to bear. The truth of the matter is perhaps that he had a planned course to chart and nothing and nobody would be allowed to deter him from it. So many players came to and departed from the Club, that no doubt Jim Thompson cannot even recall half of them without looking through the record books. Although perhaps strange to many Maidstone fans some of whom might even be able to tell you a player's favourite brand of beer, it is a good example that illustrates under Jim Thompson's guidance, the team was just a 'tool' with which to get a particular job done, and that the end justified the means. When the team failed to deliver it was swiftly changed. It was not important, merely a means to an end.

Dwelling on those players for a moment - because they were important and listing the players at the Club during the 1970's reads like a 'who's who' of non-League football, if nothing else. Top of the list would be Mickey Angel, for a long time the Club's record goalscorer, who was only superseded in later years by the prolific, Steve Butler. Angel, scored 129 goals for the Stones, and actually appeared at two different times for the Club, once during the mid

1960's and again around ten years later. Also in the 1970's side we find Glenn Aitkin, a midfielder who is fondly remembered by many, who seemed to score occasional, but important goals. Kenny Hill, Chris Kinnear, Brian Gregory, Glenn Coupland, are all well known non-League names, and all appeared in the Maidstone line-ups.

Despite conflicting arguments, Jim Thompson's influence at Maidstone United cannot be ignored or indeed underestimated. Jim Thompson certainly influenced much at the Club. The writer can recall one particular match that was taking place around the Christmas period, in truly appalling conditions. The match should not really have been started as puddles had already formed in several places on the ground. The match was against long-standing rivals Dartford. Maidstone were 1-0 down at half time, and the referee consulted several of the groundstaff during the break - including a gentleman named 'Ted', the head groundsman - enquiring as to whether the pitch was playable for another 45 minutes. Ted looked at the dark sky from which torrents of rain were pouring and said that he felt the pitch could only get worse. Upon hearing of this exchange, Jim Thompson, so the story goes, stormed out of his seat in the Director's box and told the unfortunate groundsman that he should keep his opinions to himself, and furthermore unless he returned to the referee and assured him that the game could continue, he would be out of a job. As it turned out, the game was restarted, although it degenerated to a farce, and Maidstone scrambled a draw. So, as far as football was concerned, Jim Thompson's intervention was justified. However, with regard to man-management, non-interference, etc., the Chairman left no one in any doubt as to where they stood.

Maidstone United moved into the 1980's, a decade during which Jim Thompson and the staff at Maidstone United would suffer the full range of emotions. A decade during which the club would take on the appearance of a volcano, beginning quietly, rumbling during the middle, and finally erupting at the end.

1977/78 Squad

Back Row, left to right . . . F. Brooks (Trainer), C. Broughton, S. Hunt, C. Hall, D. Bellotti, G. Baker, M. Wright, R. Stanifield.
Middle Row, left to right . . . H. Drury, R. Holland, J. Keirs, W. Fogarty, P. Kemp, N. Merrick, J. McVeigh, P. Jackson,
T. Dunn, D. Robinson, P. Goddard (Physiotherapist).
Front Row, left to right . . . G. Russo, S. Fraser, D. Crush, G. Coupland, B. Watling (Manager), J. Thompson (Chairman),
D. McLachlan (Assistant Manager), R. Irvine, C. Kinnear, P. Stonebridge, K. Wallace.

Looking back on the 1980's, we can see that it is in this decade that things finally began to happen for Maidstone United. Indeed, it could be said that whilst the club achieved much success on the field, events off the pitch were to prove to be more than significant in one way or another. Looking back on the club's history as a whole, it can be seen that until the 1970's, the club was amateur if not in manner, then certainly in attitude, with little potential to fulfil it's ambitions, if indeed there were any. They appeared to stumble from one period to the next, often in financial trouble, and mainly due to this, unable to field professional players (or staff), and thus not attracting the sort of crowds that they felt they deserved. Then with the arrival of Jim Thompson, things changed dramatically. He asked the question, *"do you want League football"*? Those who didn't were allowed to leave or were removed, those who did were expected to provide undying loyalty and in some cases financial input to help pay for the task facing the club.

The 1980's were to prove to be both the best and worst of times in the club's history. Success on and off the field was often a case of 'papering over the cracks'. It was also a period when for the first time the supporters began to make themselves known, to give voice to their opinions, and eventually even to doubt the communications emerging from the club. The end of the 1970's had seen the F.A. Cup successes against Exeter City and Charlton Athletic, and over £100,000 having been spent on the Athletic ground, known locally as: the 'London Road (stadium)', the 'Athletic Ground' or sometimes, 'The Maidstone Stadium'.

1979\80 saw the club win the Kent Senior Cup, the West Kent Challenge Cup and the Kent Amateur League. The team was also runners-up in the Eastern Pro-floodlit Cup. The following year, the club added the Kent County Youth Cup, displaying their commitment to youth and new, young, players. Indeed, throughout the early 1980's, there was an annual trial held, to which anyone was invited. The club was always committed to a search for new talent from the surrounding area.

The highlight of 1980/81 was the F.A. Cup victory over local rivals Gillingham. Forced to a second replay after two hard fought matches, the Stones had to travel to Priestfield for the match. Maidstone were fired up for the game. The local media featured centre-page spread, dealt with opinions and each team's merits. Gillingham and the Stones were fierce local rivals, and certainly the Maidstone supporters felt their team had something to prove. Prove it they most certainly did. Glenn Aitkin scored the first and then Frank Ovard - the Maidstone supporter's favourite - attempted an outrageous lob from around thirty yards out. Gillingham's Ron Hillyard stretched in vain but really had little hope as the ball flew into the net. The Maidstone fans were ecstatic, an outsider, as the writer virtually was at the time, would have thought their team had **won** the cup! The Gills fans were obviously disappointed, but even they could not have thought that Maidstone United fans would **still** be reminding them of that Cup defeat even to this day!

In 1981/82, having left the Southern League, Maidstone United finished a poor 16th in the Alliance Premier League. The newly formed Alliance was a product of some astute, and in the long run, clever re-organisation, in which the non-League world began to sort itself into a form of pyramid, although the word was hardly used then. Those involved, including Jim Thompson, felt that the non-League fraternity had to prove to the Football League that such a system could work if there was ever to be a realistic pattern of progress for non-League clubs. This process would eventually result in automatic promotion to the Football League, a process which Jim Thompson - who was also Chairman of the Alliance Premier League (later the Gola League and the GM Vauxhall Conference) - was instrumental in organising.

In the F.A. Trophy, Maidstone United went out to Bishop's Stortford 3-0 in the third round and lost 0-1 at home to Barking in the fourth qualifying round of the F.A. Cup. In the Alliance Premier League, it was a tale of inconsistency that ensured that a low placing was all they achieved.

(Top) Maidstone players enjoy the moment, after their F.A.Cup win over their Football League neighbours

The team - consisting of such players as the England Amateur International, Brian Thompson, the infamous goalkeeper, Dickie Guy, and Mark Newson, later to become a professional - was brilliant. They beat A.P. Leamington 4-0, Dartford 5-1 and Northwich Victoria 6-1 at home, but away lost to Boston 6-0 and to Worcester 4-1. Too many draws and not enough goals was the final verdict.

The Manager, Bill Williams, was always looking to improve the team, which Jim Thompson boasted was the 'Manchester United of non-League football'. The ex-Tottenham and England International, Peter Taylor joined the club. Certainly, as in the 1970's, the Club managed to attract the cream, of non-League players. John Bartley was a prolific scorer, and appeared for the club during two different periods, and they also boasted the almost legendary Frank Ovard. The latter was renowned for his ability to win penalties, as this ditty, taken up by Maidstone supporters in the late 1980's and 90's when they were enjoying Football League status (long after Ovard had left), illustrates;

> *I'm dreaming of a Frank Ovard,*
> *Just like the one we used to know,*
> *When the ball came over, and he fell over,*
> *And Maidstone had a penalty again*

In addition to Ovard, there was Tony Lynch, with his own unofficial 'fan club' on the terraces, known as 'the Lynch mob', Mark Golley, Mickey Joyce, Derek Richardson (a one eyed goalkeeper!), Brian Thompson, Mark Newson, Mickey Dingwall, and many more. Many names would still be familiar to most non-League fans, and if assembled as a team, they would surely give anyone a run for their money.

As the 1982/83 season unfolded, Maidstone United were 'in the frame', and Jim Thompson announced that the club would be applying to the Football League for election. In the event the Stones finished as runners-up, but were still eligible to apply.

At that time, the system required the two teams finishing at the bottom of Division 4 to apply for re-election, and be challenged for their places by the top non-League team(s) in the country. In theory therefore, non-League teams could gain League status, however in practice there was an 'old pals' agreement. Some teams were perennially applying for re-election. Hartlepool were (yet again) up for re-election, and the Stones were challenging for their place. The local Kent Messenger newspaper reported the story in detail, the Stones launched an extensive bid - some reports suggested that the whole package had cost around £1 million! Feedback was very positive, with many saying that enough was enough, that Hartlepool had enjoyed too long a period of grace, and that the time was ripe for a new club, such as Maidstone.

It was shortly before the voting that two big clubs, supposedly Liverpool and Everton (although this was never confirmed), changed their bids and voted for Hartlepool. Maidstone lost out, although as minor consolation, it was reported that they had polled 26 votes, more than anyone had ever accumulated before without actually being elected. Jim Thompson, Bill Williams, and the Maidstone fans were devastated. The Club had come so close to fulfilling the 'dream', only for it to be snatched away at the last moment.

The job of picking oneself up from disappointment is always a very difficult task, however, Jim Thompson picked up the club as whole, and assured them that the only way to react was to fight back and strengthen the club's position. The next season they must improve and win the Alliance League. This task was to prove to be difficult enough, but the pitch they played on was put under more pressure when Rugby League football was introduced to the stadium. It was an ambitious move, especially as the game had it's roots in the north of England.

The Rugby Club, named Kent Invicta, played it's first match in August 1983 against a Cardiff side in front of around 1,800 spectators. The stadium also saw over 2,000 attend for the visit of the famous St Helens. The Kent Team boasted some famous names, such As Mark Elia and Gary Freeman, both of whom went on to play for the New Zealand Rugby League side. However, the rugby only enjoyed limited success, for there were always financial difficulties. After one season the club was sold off and moved to Southend United's ground at Roots Hall. The rugby venture was one of several during the 1970's and 80's, to provide some alternative entertainment at the stadium, greyhound racing and squash were others that were introduced. Jim Thompson realised that football no longer enjoyed the indulgence of the community, and that Clubs had to look at ways of not only raising extra revenue, but also of giving something back to the local populace. At the time, the idea was fairly new, however, many League Clubs now offer such sporting and social facilities to the local community.

Back to the football, and Maidstone United took the Alliance League by storm, winning 6-0 against Telford United in the final game to lift the Championship. Again they applied for election to the Football League, although this time the campaign was not so high profile, and again they were denied a place, this time polling only 22 votes.

Around this time Thompson was 'ousted' from the club by a boardroom coup. Jim Thompson was away in the U.S.A. at the time, and when he returned, he found that Maidstone United now had a new Chairman in Cyril Nicholls, the former vice-Chairman. Bemused Maidstone Supporters first heard of the news in the local press, on the 10th February 1984, when the Kent Messenger reported, *"Chairman toppled in Club coup"*. Jim Thompson immediately applied for, and obtained a temporary injunction in the High Court. This injunction, served at a less than amicable board meeting, prevented the 'new' board from using the shares allotted to them whilst Jim Thompson was away.

The High Court Hearing heard that the coup had arisen due to a row with Jim Thompson at a previous board meeting where he had wanted to delay the calling in of debts owed by the Rugby League Club. The Court found in favour of Jim Thompson, however it insisted that an immediate audit was done, and that all club accounts be returned to the registered offices of the Stones from the offices of Adverkit International, a company owned by Mr Thompson. Jim Thompson complied with this ruling, however, the first seeds of doubt had been sown and those involved in the coup left the Club. Jim Thompson ensured that never again would anyone be able to 'takeover', unless he wanted them to. Later, those involved in the coup, made allegations concerning their worries over the effect of Rugby on the playing surface at the club, possible share-dealing and tax provisions.

Nearly all of those involved accused Jim Thompson of attempting to run the club alone, and ignoring the views and wishes of the majority. Mr Jim Hilton, a board member of the board at that time, was quoted as saying;

"Soon after I went on [the board] *it was apparent to me that there was only one person who had a say in the club and that was Jim Thompson".*

Today, such a revelation might not cause too much surprise, although it's hardly the best method of running a club. What may have come as more of a surprise was the fact that the books of the club were at the offices of Adverkit International, Jim Thompson's Company. It is also fairly safe to presume that the books were not a million miles away from Jim Thompson's own personal office. The reader must surely ask, is this a normal business practice? If one searched the home of the Manchester United Chairman, for instance, would one find the Club's books there? One would hope not. And how long had the books been at Adverkit International? Did Jim Thompson remove them from the Club whilst he was in the U.S.A. or had they been there for some time? It is reasonable to assume that they were there because he had control over them and wanted no one else to see them - why? What secrets did they hide? These and other questions spring to mind, and obviously are hardly likely to elicit an answer so long after the event. But it does illustrate the way Jim Thompson worked and his almost obsessive desire for secrecy, that would later become more apparent.

Following the Club's failure to get elected to the League, Bill Williams, the Manager, went to South Africa. He took the disappointment even harder than Jim Thompson, and disillusionment with the Football League establishment and the way they ran the game were cited as reasons. Whilst in Africa, Bill Williams discovered a young goalkeeper named Bruce Grobelaar, who would later go onto fame and fortune with the very successful Liverpool team of the late 80's. Bill was instrumental in helping Grobelaar to a place with the Vancouver Whitecaps in Canada and Crewe Alexander in England. Grobelaar was soon noticed, was signed by Liverpool, and went on to become a regular for the reds, whilst also playing International football for Zimbabwe.

In January 1985, Jim Thompson recruited the charismatic Barry Fry from Barnet. Fry had been a Manchester United apprentice, England schoolboy International, and a player with several other clubs including Bolton, Luton and Leyton Orient, as well as non-League Gravesend, where he was Captain. Fry, who as Manager of Barnet had achieved much the same at the North London club that Jim Thompson had at Maidstone, swept into the Stones set-up with a breath of humorous fresh air. He was loud and flash, and at the time could have been described as a poor man's non-League version of Malcolm Allison. He arrived with his *"Quick wit, expensive suits and 24 carat adornments"* . Barry Fry stayed for just over a year at Maidstone United. A year during which the team slumped into the bottom half of the table, much to the annoyance of the supporters, who demanded a public showdown with both the Manager and the Chairman present. Before the meeting could take place, Jim Thompson shut down the supporter's Club, run by the supporter's Association, which effectively ensured that organisation folded as well. It was yet another case of the Chairman ridding the field of an 'obstacle', that he perceived as an threat, real or imagined, to his dream. The showdown meeting did take place, and there was much frank talk. Barry Fry 'fielded' a number of questions from supporters, questions that were directed at Jim Thompson, whom it could be seen, was visibly annoyed at some of the bluntness of the questioning. The Chairman also directed criticism at the local Media, something that later on would become a regular occurrence.

Barry Fry eventually left the club on April 1st, 1986, having resigned. Although he had gone, the supporters were to remember him with a humorously cruel song, which went....

"He's fat, he's round, he tried to take us down, Barry Fry, Barry Fry"!

True the team had slumped to a low position in the table, but the official reason for Fry's departure was allegedly because Jim Thompson wanted him to become General Manager at the Club, leaving team matters to someone else. Later, Barry Fry stated: *"I went there in the belief that they wanted me as a football manager....I would like to think that I did well on the commercial side and in all honesty not so well on the football front. It was certainly a learning experience..."*

Fry returned to Barnet where he continued as though he had never been away. However, despite taking the Club into the Football League in the early 1990's, Fry had numerous and much publicised 'bust ups' with the Chairman there - Stan Flashman - and eventually left for Southend United, and later Birmingham City.

Following Barry Fry's departure, the club went through a brief re-organisational period, which saw the return of Bill Williams from Africa as Manager. Within two years, the Club was turned upside down as the Stones went into the late 1980's, a period which was the beginning of the end.

Barry Fry packed his bags and left, after little more than a year at London Road.

CHAPTER 6

THE END OF THE 80'S

At the beginning of the 1986 season, Jim Thompson broke the news that Maidstone United would be selling the London Road Stadium to MFI, the furniture giants. There are two principal stories as to why the Club decided to do this, the reader must decide which is nearer to the truth, if any.

The first theory claims that the Club decided that they needed to upgrade the stadium to meet Football League standards, in the event that they got the chance to apply for election again. Estimates were called for and to the shock of the Club, they found that far from being in a position to improve on the ground, there were indications that what already stood was badly in need of repair. The cost of repair and improvement was so high that it was felt that selling the ground and moving elsewhere was the only viable option. On top of this, it appeared that the Bank was becoming impatient over the Club's debt and was making noises about recovery.

The second theory is that Jim Thompson and the board decided that a move to an out of town sight, incorporating a leisure and sporting complex, was to become the right move for many clubs, and that Maidstone United should be at the vanguard of such a movement.

There are other theories, all more or less versions of the above two. The first is plausible in that it reflects the attitude of Banks toward football clubs, and that the stand above the terracing was actually demolished in the hurricane that hit Kent and the South-east in 1987. The second theory, in retrospect, fits in nicely with what Jim Thompson planned for the future of the Club following their stay at Dartford. It is certainly the one that he would admit to, as it paints him as the generous and public spirited figure that he wished to be perceived as. The truth is probably a mixture of the two.

To many supporters though, the shock was very great, and almost unimaginable. There were supporters who had watched the team for decades, and to them the Club's decision was unforgivable. However, appeasement was achieved, at least to some extent, when details of a 10,000 all seater-stadium within a multi-faceted complex was announced. The concept was new and exciting and would surely herald the dawn of a new era for the Stones.

However, in early 1987, Borough Councillors in Allington, near Maidstone, reacted to rumours that the new complex was planned for land over which they had control. They vowed to fight any plans to site the complex there, and in doing so created a trend, that was given the name "N.I.M.B.Y."s (Not In My Back Yard), and would continue throughout the area until the club's demise.

On the field, Maidstone United had progressed through to the 1st round proper of the F.A. Cup, to face Watford. On route they had made hard work of beating both Southwick and Kent rivals Welling United, both of whom took the Stones to a second game.

A young John Barnes in action during the F.A.Cup-tie at Watford

For the Watford match, the club successfully roused all the supporters, a special train was laid on, and party accessories such as streamers, hats, and scarves were made available. It all appeared slightly too contrived, but the Stones bandwagon was rolling and the club were determined to create a party-type atmosphere regardless of the result, whatever happened, a great day **was** to be had by all.

The day, 10th January 1987, turned out to be better than expected, nearly 4,500 Maidstone fans made the trip to swell the crowd to over 15,000. The Stones fans created a lot of noise, especially when Tony Lynch put them ahead! In the end, Maidstone were beaten 3-1 by the League team, however, they were by no means disgraced, and the fans and the Club had a great day to remember. In terms of publicity however, once again the cup exploits of other 'more fashionable' non-League clubs overshadowed that of the Stones.

Maidstone's squad was one of the best for years, and included such names as Malcolm Stewart, Steve Galloway, George Torrance, Tony Pamphlett, Phil Handford and Steve Butler, all well known in either professional or semi-professional circles. Steve Butler had been signed from Brentford, where he had only made a few appearances, and would go on to become Maidstone's top scorer two years in a row before leaving to play for Cambridge United and Watford.

Meanwhile, in February 1987, Jim Thompson revealed the plans for the complex, which included a multi-sports area, a 10,000 all-seater stadium, a sports injury clinic, and a 300 seat restaurant. This was to be at Bunyards Farm, Allington, just outside Maidstone. The whole deal would cost £3 million, and relied on the MFI group receiving planning permission for the football ground. This was refused in April 1987, and presented both parties with a headache. Mr Thompson accused those who had turned down the application of being like characters from Alice in Wonderland. Additionally, Maidstone United were having problems with the site they had chosen, and were further dismayed when the Council's Highways Department, insisted that a nearby railway bridge would have to be widened, at a cost to the club of between £1-£2 million!

By this time, MFI had appealed against the refusal to grant planning permission and had won, and thus demanded access to the stadium. Maidstone United were suddenly facing a bill of £4 million to finance the building of a stadium which they had budgeted £3 million for. With the weight of local opposition and the restrictions imposed by the Council, the club had no choice but to abandon Bunyards Farm. It is this point which should be particularly noted, for it is in direct conflict with the often posed question of why the club sold the ground without first having anywhere to go. They certainly did (appear) to have somewhere to go, and contracts were drawn up, but these were reliant on planning permission being granted. The failure of that option had nothing to do with the Club, but a lot to do with the local residents and various politicians involved. Sadly, for the club, they set a precedent for dissent which was copied elsewhere in the borough every time the Club thought it had found a site on which to build.

The last match at the London Road stadium was played on April 23rd 1988 against Stafford Rangers. The crowd was big and many 'dignitaries' came to pay their last respects to the stadium, including David Sadler, the one time Maidstone schoolboy who had found fame and fortune with Manchester United.

SEASON 1987-88   100 PENCE

Maidstone United F.C.

Saturday, 23rd April, 1988
K.O. 3.00 p.m.
Maidstone United
vs.
Stafford Rangers

Sponsors for 1987/88
WIMPEY Welcome Home

Souvenir Edition No:

For full match report see the KENT MESSENGER & EXTRA   1077

Bill Williams, the Manager at the time wrote in the programme that day: *"There are difficult days ahead"*. In retrospect, Bill's words are a huge understatement, for the Stones' problems had only just begun.

Whilst the London Road stadium was being levelled by MFI, Jim Thompson was searching for a ground.

The end of the London Road ground......

....to be replaced by another MFI building.

(Lower photo: Dave Twydell)

With the Bunyards Farm deal having fallen through, he found that he had a club with nowhere to play. He approached nearly every club in the surrounding area, including Ashford, Gravesend and even Gillingham. Some Stones fans hated the thought of their team playing at Priestfield, and apparently so did certain people at Gillingham. Despite a promise to rebuild the Gordon Road stand for them, the Gills declined the Stone's application to groundshare. The official reason was, they said, that as they too intended to move (which they still havn't done!), it was pointless inviting the Stones to groundshare. Many connected with Maidstone United though felt that the real reasons had more to do with the long term rivalry between the two clubs than anything else.

It was ironic then, that within 3 years of the Stones demise, Gillingham, their supposed move to a new ground 'on ice' following Council disapproval, were placed into the hands of the liquidators. A countywide appeal was sent out for fans to turn up and help. Many in Maidstone resented this, why should we help they asked, what did Gillingham do to help us? A fair point.

Ashford was considered too far, Gravesend and Chatham not to League standard, which left Dartford. And thus it was to old rivals Dartford that Jim Thompson went, with a deal to a temporary groundsharing arrangement, until the Stones could find a new ground in Maidstone. Dartford agreed and the Stones were in business for 1988/89.

The team began the 1988/89 season in fine form, beating Cheltenham and then Wycombe 4-0 and 3-2 away respectively, before thumping Altrincham 7-2 at Watling Street, Dartford, in front of just 624. For many Maidstone United supporters, the selling off of the Athletic Ground was bad enough, but to actually move 25 miles away to Dartford was unspeakable. Many fans simply didn't realise the complications that Jim Thompson had suffered in relation to Bunyards Farm, and accused him of selling off the Stadium without having anywhere to go. There was a sizeable drop in the number of Stones fans that watched the team at Dartford, even though the club laid on a special bus service to ferry the fans to and from the games. In fact during the season, the year they won promotion to the GM Vauxhall

Conference, not once did the Stones manage to attract more than 3,000 fans to Watling Street for a League match. The biggest home crowd that season was 2,821 for an F.A. Cup replay with Reading.

But the Stones were beginning to show real form. With players such as Noel Ashford, Mark 'Smokey' Gall, Steve Butler and Ken Charlery, Maidstone were pretty formidable. At Dartford, Welling were beaten 3-0, Northwich Victoria 4-1 and Yeovil 5-0. Away from home, Kidderminster were trounced 6-3, Boston 4-1 and the now defunct Newport County 2-1.

Although Maidstone were in the top 4 or 5 for most of the season, there was a real 'danger' that they could win the Championship. This was something that Jim Thompson had not planned on, especially as he knew that Watling Street was woefully short of reaching League standards.

Not everyone was happy with the Stones playing at Dartford!

With three games to go, the Stones were top of the Conference having just beaten Northwich 4-1. With Jim, as the GMVC Chairman, having successfully negotiated automatic promotion to the Football League, Scarborough and Lincoln had already taken advantage - or become victims - of the system and now the very distinct possibility of the 'dream' being fulfilled for the Stones was drawing very close.

It was in fact on 1st May 1989, that Maidstone United clinched promotion. They were involved in the Kent Senior Cup Final, ironically enough at Gillingham's Priestfield stadium, when the word went round that Enfield had beaten the only team able to catch them, Kettering, 1-0.

(Left) The last 'home' match as a non-League team.

The celebrations were capped by the fact that they beat Welling to win the Cup, and still had two Conference matches, away at Barnet and Runcorn, to play!

The Stones players celebrate their promotion to the Football League.

With the GM Vauxhall Conference Championship trophy held aloft, the team rode through the streets of Maidstone on an open topped bus, cheered on by about 2,000 supporters. The then Mayor, Jeremy Hindle, at the Civic Reception, promised that the town would fulfil it's obligation to, *"bring the Stones home"*. The phrase would become the watchword of a long and frustrating campaign to return the Club to the County town, fought against a mountain of petty local politics, Council bureaucracy, and the ever present NIMBY's.

For Jim Thompson and Maidstone United, the more practical problems of preparing for the Football League occupied the immediate future. John Still, the Man who had successfully taken the Stones to the Championship, declined the one year contract offered by the Chairman, saying that he wanted a longer one, and reluctantly resigned. Jim Thompson therefore had to sign a Manager, and quickly. The man he chose would have to re-sign all the previous part-time players as full professionals, get them training, and prepare them for full time football.

Whilst this was happening, the Chairman had to endure masses of new regulations regarding the ground, the Hillsborough stadium tragedy had only just happened and the Football League was under severe pressure to ensure that such an event was never repeated. They therefore insisted on Maidstone United implementing many improvements to the Watling Street ground. Upon seeing the miles of wire fencing and new crash barriers, all painted in yellow, one fan was heard to say, *"Blimey, welcome to Colditz"*. The fans of the Stones' new landlords, Dartford, were even more unimpressed. They saw the vast areas of yellow and black paint which had been used to decorate their ground, and declared, via their fanzine, *"Light at the end of the tunnel"*, that Maidstone United had in fact come to take over rather than share the ground. So vociferous did the complaints become, in fact, that the Dartford board asked Maidstone United to repaint parts of the ground in the black, white and red of their club.

A number of improvements were needed to bring the Watling Street ground up to the required standards.
(Photo: John Robinson - Soccer Bookshelf)

It has been seen that the Maidstone United story is littered with controversy, and even claiming their right to a place in the Football League caused a stir. Darlington, the club whom the Stones were to replace, claimed that Watling Street was, *"another Hillsborough waiting to happen"*. They also claimed that the ground's capacity did not come up to the Football League's regulations, a protest that was easily ignored when one considered some grounds of some clubs already in the League. At one stage, Darlington even threatened to take their case to the High Court and get an injunction to stop Maidstone United competing. But, in truth, the whole protest sounded nothing more than a severe case of sour grapes. Ironically, one of Darlington's founders was C S Craven, who was also a founder of Maidstone United (see Chapter 1)!

Another threat came from closer to home, in the shape of Vic Jobson, the Chairman at Southend United. There had been a long-running feud between Vic Jobson and Jim Thompson, and there were rumours that the two had fallen out way back over the Rugby League Club, which moved from Maidstone to Southend. Essentially it seemed that Southend had agreed to purchase the club when it was clear that it was not a success at Maidstone. Trouble began when money promised was never paid, and the argument had festered ever since.

Vic Jobson claimed that Watling Street would not meet League requirements and questioned the club's security of tenure. With apparently more than just a little personal malice against the Maidstone Chairman, he argued that Darlington had more right to remain in the Football League. His views erupted at the League meeting for Associate Members. Jim Thompson was required to attend the Football League Headquarters and meet, greet and make his acceptance speech to the other Chairmen of the Third and Fourth Division clubs.

It is alleged that Vic Jobson attempt to disrupt Jim Thompson's speech, and was eventually ejected from the room having been ruled out of order. Not a man to take such a snub lying down, Vic Jobson's discontent would re-emerge later in the season when the two teams met on the field.

Meanwhile, Keith Peacock had been appointed Team Manager, and he began the task of signing the players on professional terms, and Mark 'Smokey' Gall became the first player ever to sign Professional forms for the club. In addition, Peacock also had to train and prepare the players for the Football League, and had the unpleasant task of sorting out the 'chaff from the wheat ' - getting rid of those players whom he didn't want in his squad.

Keith Peacock, is one of those rarities in football, a genuine man. He had been a player at Charlton Athletic, and then followed the exodus of players to the U.S.A. in the early 1970's, joining the N.A.S.L. when it had money to burn. He had returned to the U.K. and was appointed the Manager of Maidstone's rivals, Gillingham, but had left when ignominiously sacked. Most observers felt he was hard done by. He then went to Queens Park Rangers as assistant Manager, until enticed away by Jim Thompson. One of Keith's first appointments, was that of Tommy Taylor, once a player at West Ham, as his assistant.

The League fixture list was announced, and Maidstone United were drawn away to Peterborough United for their first Football League Match. The supporters and club made itself ready to return, poignantly perhaps, to London Road. London Road, Peterborough that is.

Keith Peacock

The Stone's inaugural Football League match was played at Peterborough United on Saturday 19th August 1989. To the eternal anger of the writer, this match was missed due to an administrative error relating to the away travel, which ensured that around twenty Stones fans missed the game. Basically, the coach driver was not informed that he had to stop where these unfortunates

were waiting, and refused to do so when other supporters realised the error and told him.

It appeared that he was fairly obnoxious for the whole journey and was later sacked by the bus company after many fans complained. Although this did nothing to appease those that were stranded, Maidstone United did grant complimentary travel for the next match.

At Peterborough the pre-match was marked with presentations by the home Club to the Stones' Chairman, Jim Thompson's wife, and in the programme, Peterborough wrote; *"They* [Maidstone United] *are all approaching it* [The Football League] *with the right attitude. The balloons will go up today to welcome Maidstone United into the Football League".*

And indeed, up they went. Maidstone supporters made up around 2,500 of the 6,522 crowd. Sadly, the Stones didn't manage to win the game, beaten by a solitary goal to spoil the party. But, Maidstone had begun their Football League lives, uninterrupted by protests from Southend, or High Court Injunctions from Darlington. Jim Thompson had delivered his promise of Football League status, and even though the Club didn't have a ground of their own, such things were forgotten in the excitement of the moment.

It has been argued by some, in retrospective, that this was the moment that Jim Thompson ought to have resigned his post as Chairman of the club. He had, after all, fulfilled the 'dream' of taking Maidstone United to the Football League, and should now step down in favour of someone else, perhaps to take an honorary position as Club President. Whilst there is some merit in this, however pedantic it might sound, it is difficult - even with hindsight -

to see just who might have taken over. The only candidate that springs to mind might have been Bill Williams, who had been the Manager and was at the time the general Manager. However, there is little doubt that Jim Thompson would have insisted on having a measure of power at the Club, and would probably have ensured that **he** could have overruled anyone else.

The next match was at Watling Street, Dartford, versus old Conference rivals, Scarborough, and marked the Stone's 'home' debut. In celebration Steve Butler smashed home a hat-trick in a 4-1 demolition of the visitors, before a good crowd of 3,372. Maidstone United had begun and had now announced their arrival. That early League success was offset by an early exit from the League Cup by Cambridge United, and a string of League defeats, punctuated only by a stirring and totally unexpected 3-2 away victory at Grimsby Town. In their first 14 League matches, the Stones won just 5 games, lost 7 and drew 2. Whilst it wasn't the worst record in the world, it ensured that Maidstone were down in the wrong half of the table.

The crowds too were disappointingly low. Although 3,762 turned up for the game against Burnley, about 2,000 were from the North, which reflected the Club's ability only to attract less than 2,000 to Dartford. The question of the Club's ground also re-emerged as many old supporters refused point blank to travel to Dartford to watch the Stones. They argued that Jim Thompson had sold the team down the river and that the club had no right to even call themselves Maidstone United, unless they played in the town. Dartford's supporters were also unhappy with the groundsharing arrangement. The Dartford fanzine, *'Light at the end of the tunnel'*, repeatedly bemoaned the fact that Maidstone United seemed to be taking over their ground, and that Jim Thompson had plans to take over the Dartford Club itself and merge it with the Stones. Most Maidstone fans did agree that there did seem to be an abundance of yellow and black paint on the revamped ground, although no one really took much notice of the takeover accusations, dismissing them with a derisory, *"Why would Jim Thompson want a club like Dartford anyway"*.

Nicky Johns

Mark Beeney

The fortunes of the team on the pitch, led to the first controversy of the season, when Keith Peacock brought in goalkeeper Nicky Johns to the Club, on loan, for the away game with Scunthorpe, and dropped Mark Beeney. Beeney was a local lad who had been signed from Gillingham, having only made one appearance for them. He had been ever-present in the Championship winning side of the previous season, and had been set to join Coventry City as an understudy to the Sky Blues veteran Steve Ogrizivic.

Keith Peacock however persuaded Mark that his future was with Maidstone United and that playing in the Stone's inaugural Football League season would benefit him much more.

Maidstone's poor early season form had seen other casualties too. Tony Pamphlett had scored an outrageous own goal in the match versus Cambridge and never played again in the League for Maidstone. Mark Beeney, the goalkeeper that day, had also attracted some of the blame for that goal, albeit somewhat unfairly. But Keith Peacock decided that Mark need a jolt and returned to Q.P.R. for the veteran Johns. He played against Scunthorpe and did fairly well, but against Lincoln in the next match he was injured, and Beeney returned. The Nicky Johns story, would continue, and although temporarily over, he was to return later in the season.

The influence of Vic Jobson then re-emerged. It appeared that Southend United had contacted Maidstone and informed them, in no uncertain terms, that not one supporter from Maidstone would be allowed into their Roots Hall stadium unless a card-carrying member of the Club. As luck would have it, Maidstone United **did** have a membership scheme, although it carried virtually no benefits at all. The club ran a small piece in the programme for the Lincoln match;

"IMPORTANT
Would Supporters wishing to follow the club to Southend United this Saturday, please note that for all areas, standing or seated, visiting supporters must carry their own club's membership card".

The result of this was that the club was deluged with membership applications. As it turned out, Southend United didn't check to see whether supporters were carrying cards or not, and denied ever demanding they must. Many Maidstone United supporters felt that this was a ruse by Jim Thompson to raise some money quickly. Others weren't so sure. Vic Jobson had conducted an interview with the Kent Messenger, which appeared before the day of the match, stating that Chairman Jim Thompson and his board of Directors would **not** be allowed into the boardroom at Southend and would **not** be allocated seating in the Directors box, which was normally given to visiting Club officials. The message was clear, Maidstone United were not welcome. As if that was not clear enough, the matchday programme underlined the fact....

"The state of the Dartford ground has caused much comment and criticism and it is highly questionable whether it is up to Football League standard. Blues Chairman, Vic Jobson, certainly does not think so and with both the dubious safety level of the main stand, the lack of proper segregation of rival fans and the lack of entrances and exits to the ground, it seems a valid point. Their long term aim is to return to Maidstone and a new stadium which will dispel all protests as to whether they deserve their status".

The Comments, obviously influenced and possibly even written by Vic Jobson himself, were outrageous. They not only took issue with Maidstone United, but also with the Football League who had inspected and passed the Watling Street stadium. Clearly whoever had penned the piece had **not** visited Watling street, as one of the main complaints by supporters **was** the segregation of rival fans and the yards of fencing through which a good view was impossible.

Maidstone United arrived at Southend and were given an extraordinary welcome. Jim Thompson and his board were ignored and shuttled off to a far corner of the main stand, whilst the fans were subjected to some of the most officious policing anyone had ever experienced. The Police behaviour was surprising, even when compared to some rough handling at bigger Clubs.

Arrests and ejections were random and unsolicited, whilst protests fell on deaf ears. But the Stones had the last laugh on two counts, for Steve Butler snatched the only goal of the game, and although it took some heroic goalkeeping from the reinstated Beeney to win the points, win they did.

Maidstone United complained to the Football League about their treatment, both in the ground and in respect of the comments in the programme, and Vic Jobson and Southend were disciplined. Thus, although a minor but interesting distraction, Vic Jobson's tactics had backfired on him. Not only had Maidstone United received an unexpected but welcome boost to their coffers via sales of membership cards, but the Stones had beaten Southend to take the points!

The final chapter occurred later in the season when Southend visited Watling Street. Vic Jobson, perhaps in a petty but dramatic statement regarding the safety of the edifice, refused to sit in the Watling Street main stand, and joined the Southend supporters on the terraces rather than 'risk' the supposed frailty of the Directors box, where he would be once more witness to a Maidstone victory over his club.

By December, the Stones had improved their League position, although they were out of the F.A. Cup, after losing to Exeter City in torrential rain in the West country after a replay. They were now set for their 'Match of the season', against local Kent rivals, Gillingham. The prospect of the first all Kent League match had appealed to the public imagination, and the contest was the talk of the County. Neither Gillingham or Maidstone boasted troublemakers, but that did not stop a few idiots issuing threats of trouble. Some Gillingham fans did actually visit Maidstone town centre with a spray can, and leave their messages of hate and violence, but on the day nothing actually happened.

Steve Butler

The police had imposed a safety restriction on the size of the crowd, of 10,000, however it was generally accepted that this was a fairly relaxed restriction, and although the game was held at 11.00 in the morning of December 26th, there were queues around the Priestfield stadium from about 8.30. Unofficial figures put the final attendance at about 14,500! The game itself was an anti-climax after all the pre-match hype. In fact it wasn't a very good game, the players were too tense and mistakes too frequent.

Mark 'Smokey' Gall

Gall, a legend at Maidstone, formed a formidable scoring partnership with Steve Butler

But there was plenty of incident, especially in the second half. Maidstone United had sent their fans into raptures with two goals, one in the first period and another early in the second, against a tentative Gillingham. Steve Butler and Mark Gall both scored, signalling the start of a huge party for the 4,000 or so Maidstone fans at the town end of the ground. The Gills then went onto the offensive and began to get back into the match, but the Stones defence relied on measures of competence, luck, and the goalkeeping of Mark Beeney.

Halfway through the second half, the referee awarded a penalty for an infringement in the Maidstone penalty area, and Gill's Steve Lovell prepared to take the kick. As a penalty kick there have been better, but there have also been a lot worse; Beeney hurled himself across the goal to tip the ball away. The Maidstone fans celebrated yet again, surely the Gods were smiling on the Stones that day? The Maidstone fans taunted Gillingham's faithful that their club had sold Beeney to Maidstone, and didn't they regret it now? The thought must also have crossed a few minds of those in the Gillingham Directors box.

The game had one last dramatic scenario to play out, and that involved the Gillingham Captain, Alan Walker. With around ten minutes to go, and Gillingham looking for two goals to save not only the match but also their reputations, Walker flung himself at a far post cross. He connected and the ball did indeed fly into the net, but Walker had forgot to apply the brakes and ended up at the foot of the post having collided with it. It seemed that at one point he had swallowed his tongue and only swift work by those on the spot saved him. He was out for around two minutes and amazingly got up to continue the match. He later admitted that the last three or four minutes of the game were a blur. But, despite Alan Walker's heroics, the Stones held on for their most famous and cherished win of the season. With all the celebrating going on it was difficult to remind oneself that it had been a League game worth in real terms, just three points. For the Maidstone faithful, Christmas was especially sweet that year.

"Here
We
Go"

The loyal band of supporters at Torquay United.

Following such a prestigious match as that, it was always going to be difficult to get the team's feet back on the ground, however defeat at Torquay on the last day of 1989 did the trick in no uncertain terms.

But the players were now beginning to perform a lot better, and they bounced back to thrash Aldershot 5-1 on New Year's Day at Watling Street. The victory heralded the start of a 17 game run during which the team suffered just one defeat.

Around March 1990, Mark Beeney found himself in dispute with Keith Peacock. The Manager was given the option to buy Nicky Johns, which he took up, and Beeney found himself out of the team. The introduction of Nicky Johns was one of the most controversial signings that Keith Peacock made, although at the time he must have felt he was simply strengthening the squad. By replacing Mark Beeney, the fan's favourite and a local boy to boot, Johns found himself the target of the Maidstone crowd, who felt that he was not only past it, but not as good as Beeney. In actual fact, Johns was a fine reflex goalkeeper, who had played at Millwall and had become something of a legend at Charlton Athletic before going on to play for Tampa Bay Rowdies in the U.S.A., then Sheffield United and QPR.

It was clear that Keith Peacock knew Johns quite well, having been involved at three of the same clubs as him. Nicky Johns was to establish himself in the side as far as the Club was concerned, but he never overcame the fans, who cruelly jeered both his name when it was announced in the team line-up and the man himself whenever he appeared. Mark Beeney was loaned out to Aldershot for a period, did quite well, and managed to make it back to Maidstone and a regular first team place by the end of the season.

Suddenly, the team had found itself up amongst the promotion places, such a feat had never been planned for, and would be a major coup. A disheartening defeat at Wrexham (4-2), ended the run and although the Stones recovered to win their next two games, signs of pressure were beginning to show. Gillingham arrived on Easter Monday to inflict a 1-0 defeat in a bruising and bad tempered affair, followed by a disastrous 4-2 defeat away at Hartlepool. The Stones finished with a flourish though, and beat Torquay 5-1 at home, drew 0-0 with York away and on a lovely sunny day in early May trounced Carlisle United 5-2 to ensure themselves a place in the play-offs.

The Club like most others in a new League had publicly said that of course they had planned for consolidation rather than to take the Division by storm, although it is reasonable to assume that Jim Thompson felt the Club were big enough to compete at a higher level, and that they might do well in their first year.

The play-off was a two legged affair with the winner going to a final match at Wembley. It was a source of acute annoyance that Maidstone United had never played beneath the twin towers, however here was as good a chance as any. The team they faced was Cambridge United, who had turned out to be their bogey team for the season. The 'U's had dumped Maidstone out of the League Cup at the first attempt, and in fact Maidstone had only taken 1 point from them all season, a hard fought draw that had Tony Pamphlett not put through his own net minutes from time might have registered 3 points for the Stones.

But Cambridge always gave the Stones a hard game, and once again it was the same at the Abbey stadium. Cambridge scored first to ensure that the Stones had to chase the rest of the game. It was Mark Gall who scored the equaliser, with barely five minutes to go. The away section echoed to the sound of Maidstone's fans celebrations for almost twenty minutes after the game had finished.

The return leg was an evening kick-off, and played on 16th May 1990. The ground was packed, creating a new ground record, for Maidstone, of 5,008, and the atmosphere was terrific as the two teams took the field in the warm spring evening. The match turned out to be a tale of Maidstone pressure as the Stones 'camped' in the Cambridge half, putting the visitors under all sorts of pressure.

Maidstone had their chances, hitting bar, post and legs, but the luck and a brave goalkeeping display from John Vaughan kept Maidstone out. With barely ten minutes left, Dion Dublin broke away and scored twice to end Maidstone's Wembley dreams. To be so near and then have the tie snatched from their grasp in such a fashion was cruel indeed.

However, Maidstone had done incredibly well. Upon moving to Dartford, they were given little chance of the GM Vauxhall Conference title, being so far from Maidstone, the experts predicted that it would all be too much for the Stones. It wasn't. Much the same argument was raised when considering them as potential Division 4 Champions, and despite a lack of decent crowds, the team had done astonishingly well. Although they had exited the League Cup in a short sharp fashion, their F.A.Cup matches had taken them to the 2nd round. They had also done well in the Leyland DAF Cup, thumping Third Division Northampton 4-2 via a stunning Mark 'Smokey' Gall hat-trick, beaten Colchester United 2-1, Mansfield Town then in the third division 2-1 away, Exeter City 2-0 at home before bowing out to a very good Notts County team in the regional semi-final by the only stunning goal of the game. Early on in the season they had won the fairly meaningless GM Vauxhall Conference Championship Shield, easily beating Telford 2-0, and ended the season by beating Gillingham 1-0 for a second time at Priestfield to win the Facit Kent Senior Cup.

Disappointment at the Failure to beat Cambridge in the play-off was tempered by the fact that the United then went on to beat Stockport County at Wembley to win promotion.

Meanwhile, Jim Thompson had other duties to perform, a fact of which he reminded everyone in the match programme for the Carlisle game: *"I am sure many of you must be wondering what there is for the Chairman to do.....the answer is plain and simple. Locate a new ground, build a new stadium and sports complex worthy of the Club and it's new found stature in the Football League, and I assure you that my office and staff spend every hour of every day working towards that end."*

That may have been so, but it was less than reassuring to the supporters to know that a site had not yet been found, and in fact, the statement reminded everyone that the Stones **still** had no home. The local Council appeared to be doing very little to fulfil their promise to bring the Stones home and seemed to resist almost every overture made by the Club. The fans had even adapted the words to a song that was regularly sung on the terraces, that contained the lines:

"We are Maidstone, We are Maidstone, Super Maidstone, from nowhere, no one likes us, no one likes us, the council hate us, we don't care".

Whilst the 1989/90 successfully ran, the team's performance had ensured that the ground finding problems were at best, temporarily forgotten, or at worst on the back burner. The following season brought the problem sharply back into focus. The problem was heightened by the fact that the supporters' fanzines regularly covered the fact that the Stones had no ground, that they hated Dartford and that the Club didn't seem to be doing too much.

Fanzines were independently produced magazines, written, edited, produced, published and distributed by the fans. They had been around since the late 1970's, gained momentum in the 1980's, and established themselves during the latter part of that decade. Supporters who previously had no say, now had the opportunity to say what they thought about the club they supported.

Maidstone United fans decided to set up fanzines when the club entered the Football League. The first was called, *"The Spirit of London Road"*, an offering with a great title, but sadly a short life span. This title was followed by, *"The Foundation Stone"*, *"Show me the way to go home"* and the writer's own, *"Yellow Fever"*, which was eventually renamed, *"Golden days"*. All reported the Stones problems in various, and often humorous ways, and all were read by the Club's hierarchy. Whether they actually took much notice of the fans views is doubtful. The Club though produced their own 'fanzine' (more of a 'clubzine'), entitled *"Hailstones"*, however this didn't survive more than two issues as the fans more or less labelled it, *"a magazine from them pretending to be us"*.

CHAPTER 8

ROCKING THE BOAT

"Calm down lads"; Keith Peacock in a rare demonstrative mood.
The short reign for the manager, and Tommy Taylor (sitting) was soon to end.
Jason Lillis waits his chance to come on.

The end of season 1989/90, following the disappointment of not beating Cambridge United in the play-offs, bought renewed calls for information from the Club. The office staff consisted of Bill Williams, General Manager, Bernie and Marlene Holden, who, though working under the collective umbrella of Promotions and lottery staff appeared to have rather closer ties with Jim Thompson, Mick Mercer who had been connected with the Club for years, and according to those with an opinion, probably knew more about the workings of the Club than anyone else. Barbara Legg, was the Office Manager, and was very proud of the fact that she was the first woman ever to appear in a team photograph in the Football League yearbook. Craig Gee, a young lad who had first come to the Club as a YTS trainee, and appeared to do more or less anything that no one else fancied. These were the people who received and often fielded telephone calls, the majority, it has to be said, asking for news of developments about a new ground.

Unfortunately, Jim Thompson and the board, who later claimed that 99% of decisions were taken by Jim without any consultation with them, were apparently not in a position to let their office staff know what was happening, hence little information could therefore be passed on. So frustrating was this situation, that many simply didn't bother to try and find out anything, and preferred instead to listen to the numerous rumours floating about, and attempt to find the grain of truth behind which all rumours start. As usual Dartford supporters insisted that Jim Thompson was planning a takeover of their Club, another rumour suggested that he wanted to relocate to the bottom of a nearby chalk pit, build a stadium and rename the Club 'Kent Invicta'! From the ridiculous to the sublime claimed Maidstone United fans, however in the absence of any **real** information, rumours such as these flourished.

It later transpired that Jim Thompson **had** in fact purchased controlling shares in Dartford, but the fans were certainly not told, and none probably bothered to investigate. Whilst it did not seem as if Maidstone United would be relocating 'back to their ancestral home', as the media like to describe the situation, most Stones fans turned their attention to the delights of the World Cup Finals, currently taking place in Italy and imaginatively entitled "Italia '90".

Once the World Cup was over, Stones fans began to prepare for the coming season. Before it could begin though, Warren Barton was sold to First Division Wimbledon for £300,000. The thought of Barton moving came as no real surprise to the fans, although the price did, as he had shown, during the second half of the previous season enough class and potential to attract a number of scouts from such hallowed & prestigious bastions of football as Aston Villa, Arsenal, and 'Spurs. Well, thought most of the Maidstone fans, £300,000 would swell the coffers a bit. Unfortunately, little were they to know that the financial situation was far worse than anyone could have imagined. It was clear that Keith Peacock had no money to spend, however weren't most of the previous season's squad still around? Well yes, but many of them picked up niggling injuries, and the team was never consistently the same.

The Stones, almost by tradition rarely started well, but a 1-0 victory away at York City surprised many. The good form continued with a battling 2-2 draw with Leyton Orient in the League Cup, but from there things deteriorated. A 3-1 home defeat to Northampton and a 4-1 win by Leyton Orient in the return leg of the League Cup, rather set the pattern. Scunthorpe came and beat the Stones 1-0, although Maidstone did beat Gillingham 2-0 at Priestfield (things weren't yet **that** bad!), followed by a 4-1 thrashing of Lincoln. Maidstone went into a poor run losing 1-0 (twice) 3-1, 3-2, and 2-1 to Stockport County, Hartlepool, Walsall, Darlington and Burnley respectively.

Although in their inaugural season the team had started badly, at least they had a vague excuse in that they were getting used to the higher standard. But this time the team looked out of sorts and spiritless. Keith Peacock seemed to have lost his sparkle, whilst Mark Beeney and Nicky Johns contested and swapped the goalkeeper's shirt, although the condemnation of Nicky Johns by the fans was getting worse. By December the Stones were firmly stuck around the bottom of the table. An F.A. Cup defeat by the almost bankrupt Aldershot summed up the Stones luck.

Just as it looked like Maidstone had forgotten how to win however, they were to do just that. The season was a tale of inconsistent form. The Leyland DAF Cup was a pretty pointless competition, unless a club got through to the later stages, and it was greeted by the supporters with apathy.

It was clear that most of the competing clubs - from the Third and Fourth Division - entered the whole venture prepared to make a loss. In the main, it probably costs more to switch on the floodlights than they ever get from match receipts. In 1990/91, the preliminary games were played in an area group, and the Stones had to face Third Division Bournemouth in their first match. Just over 1000 turned up, including visiting support, to see Steve Butler, Lawrence Osbourne and Karl Elsey score to virtually guarantee passage to the next round. The Leyland DAF, for all it's lack of prestige, provided the spectacle of a winning Maidstone side, at least, for those that bothered to watch. The result seemed to steady the team as they followed this with two useful draws against Blackpool and Torquay, however away trips to Doncaster and Rochdale saw them fall back into their losing ways.

Keith Peacock must have been on the verge of despair as he surveyed his treatment room, with Dave Madden, Tony Sorrell and others struggling to get fit. It appeared that someone else at the club however had decided that enough was enough, and that something drastic had to be done. The fans were by now baying for goalkeeper Nicky John's head, who was seen as the root of all evil, and although arguably past his prime, the supporters had never given him much of a chance, and obviously didn't intend to now. Maidstone fans though had always criticised Gillingham, their hated rivals, for the manner in which Keith Peacock had been dismissed, sacked without any real reason other than just failing to steer the team to promotion. They sneered at the fact that at least Maidstone would never treat a Manager so badly. Sadly, they were very wrong. Keith Peacock was summoned, along with Assistant Manager Tommy Taylor one Monday morning to the Chairman's office, and both were promptly sacked.

Within fifteen minutes of Peacock and Taylor leaving Maidstone United's Headquarters in Maidstone, Graham Carr was seated in front of Jim Thompson and offered the job. The dismissal of messrs. Peacock and Taylor caused dismay amongst the Stones fans. Why had it been done? Jim Thompson answered them via the Kent Messenger newspaper. The fans had demanded change, he said, referring to the previous week's match, and change is what they have been given. The explanation was nonsensical, for Jim Thompson knew as well as anyone that the only man the fans wanted kicked out was Nicky Johns. In fact Thompson's excuse that he had dismissed Keith Peacock because the fans had demanded it, almost smacked of an attempt to blame them! Furthermore, since when had Jim Thompson listened to anything, let alone what the fans wanted? Quite why Keith Peacock had gone remains a mystery.

Graham Carr. His reign of Maidstone United was disliked by the fans.

Graham Carr was a totally different kettle of fish. Whereas Keith Peacock had earned a reputation as a gentleman, Graham Carr was to become known for his blunt northern opinions, insensitivity and indeed plain rudeness. An ex-marine, Graham Carr had played at one time for Dartford, had managed in non-League football, but really made his name with Third Division, Northampton Town. Some Managers appear to be 'made' for a club - as Clough did well at Nottingham Forest and Barry Fry at Barnet - so Graham Carr performed wonders at Northampton.

Having left the 'Cobblers', he made a brief sojourn to Blackpool, where he lasted all of 3 weeks, before coming to Maidstone United, undoubtedly at the request of Jim Thompson. At his first home match, his arrival at the Watling Street ground was witnessed by the writer. He swept in through the gates, waving aside several young lads asking for autographs, with a contemptuous wave of his hand. It was downhill from there on. His first action was to label the team 'unfit' and almost immediately ordered them into training half an hour earlier than they were used to.

Supporters who knew some of the players - Steve Butler liked to 'be seen' as one of the lads at the pub (though he wasn't really) and Jason Lillis and Mark Beeney enjoyed a drink with the fans - began to tell of the arduous training routine that Graham Carr tried to install. Calling upon his experience from his Marine Corps days no doubt, there were stories of assault course style training, endurance runs and tests. Terrific for muscle-bound marines and soldiers for whom stamina was all important, but not a lot of use for your average footballer. Discontent among the players was growing and strained ligaments and muscles ensured that treatment tables were even more oversubscribed at Maidstone United.

Graham Carr made no secret of the fact that he liked his defenders and central strikers to be around six feet tall and built like the sides of houses. Sadly none of Maidstone's were. Not content with upsetting the players, following a 2-0 defeat versus Southend in the Leyland DAF Cup, and a 2-0 League defeat at Northampton (that ended with a punch up on the pitch and Nicky Johns being sent off, to the delight of the travelling Stones support!), and a couple of other indifferent results, Carr turned on the fans, labelling them, *"amateur supporters at a professional Club"*. Hardly the best PR exercise in the world, and guaranteed to fill the letters columns of the local papers with angry letters from fans, saying what they thought. Finding himself with no money to buy players, Garham Carr went on a spree 'renting' players on loan to try and get the Club out of the doldrums. Maidstone fans therefore were treated to the spectacle of a succession of more or less faceless wonders who stayed for two or three matches before having to return to their Clubs.

No team can survive such a mish-mash of personnel for long, no one got to know how anyone else played as they rarely knew who would be in the team from one week to the next. To be fair to Graham Carr, he **did** bring in Bradley Sandeman, Neil Ellis and a couple of others who were purchased outright and eventually managed to make an impact.

Back on the field, The team did rally itself enough to beat rivals, Gillingham 3-1 at Watling Street, thus completing the 'double', which helped to cheer the Stones up for at least a couple of weeks. However, for a long time Maidstone United looked as though they would finish bottom of the Division, and they eventually ended up in 19th place. Gone however was the flowing and attractive football of the season before, for under Graham Carr, the Stones spent more time waiting for the ball to come out of the clouds than anything else!

The supporters of the Club had been clamouring more and more for news about a possible move back to Maidstone, and many were becoming impatient. The Maidstone United 'campaign' to return the Club to the town had been stumbling along under the title, *"Bring the Stones Home"*. Car stickers adorned, and still do, many rear windows of vehicles belonging to supporters (including a lot of 'passive' supporters). So numerous were the stickers, so it seemed, that had everyone who displayed such a sticker decided to watch the team, then they would have attracted around 50,000 to Watling Street! Sadly, the stickers seemed to be the only discernable sign that the campaign existed. Officially though the campaign was co-ordinated by a committee whose brief was purely to investigate various sites and ways of achieving the campaign's goal, but generally without coming to any conclusions.

There was a growing body of fans though, who began to get more vociferous in their questioning. *"Tell us something"*, was the message. The running (black) joke was that the Club rivalled the KGB as an information service! Eventually the Club released a full colour glossy brochure supposedly explaining what exactly had been happening, what the club's supposed policy was - that included selling the London Road stadium - and where the money had gone from the sale; what the plans for the future were, and what the Club had been doing to ensure that this became a reality. The brochure, entitled *"A new stadium for the Stones - A moving story"*, explained that in 1986/87, the Club realised that should they ever win the right to promotion to the Football League, then the London Road stadium was unlikely to qualify. The ground, it seemed, would have needed around five to £600,000 spent on it as it stood. They calculated that with the bonds required by the Football League as an entrance fee, which amounted to £200,000 and a further £250,000 for team building, then the Club would have been facing a bill of around £1 million to stay at the ground. They dismissed the idea of trying to raise the money for such a purpose adding that the ground, *"..was not big enough to generate the level of ancillary revenue needed by all football clubs"*.

From this, it seems clear that someone at the Club, probably Jim Thompson, had already decided what was wanted for the Club's future (i.e. a stadium plus a leisure complex), and that the London Road stadium was unsuitable for such expansion. The next 'choice' was that the Club remain at London Road, forget any 'dream', at least within the foreseeable future, of taking a place in the Football League, reduce the wage bill, and thus almost inevitably, lose the best players, who would obviously want to progress. Maidstone United would then probably lose their Conference place and resign themselves to playing at a lower level, in a regional league. It has been suggested that some fans might not have minded this too much. Indeed later, once the Club were in the Football League, supporters would often express their yearning for the non-League days, the camaraderie of the away trips and visits to other clubs, an atmosphere which was often absent when travelling to other League Clubs and having to deal with police constabularies who treated visiting fans almost as criminals. However one can wonder, if the Club had remained at London Road and indeed dropped from the Conference, whether those supporters would have accepted it with good grace. Probably not.

The final option, and the one that (so the brochure says) was revolutionary to say the least, was to sell the ground, *"...our only major asset"*, and, *"risk all in one great attempt to achieve entry into the Football League..."*. The argument throws up some interesting incongruities.

Jim Thompson, as Chairman of the GM Vauxhall Conference, had taken on the mantle of 'Champion' of non-League football and pushed for the Football League to accept direct promotion and relegation (albeit for just one Club) between the Conference and the League. Later he confided to the writer that, it was probably the only way that Maidstone would have ever got in. But exactly when did he realise that the London Road ground would have to go? If, as he states in the brochure, the Club had **not** planned to win promotion and that this came as a 'bombshell', why was he talking of 'one great push towards the football League', in connection with selling the ground? As we now know, a site was picked at Bunyards farm, about 2 miles further up the London Road. This would be where the new ground would be built. However, it would seem that somewhere a serious error of judgement had been made as regards local reaction. Was there no preliminary research done? Did Mr Thompson and the Club simply expect to be allowed to build a ground (and as it turns out a sports and leisure complex) without one murmur of dissent from local residents?

The bottom line is that after the first fiasco, whereby the local media released details of the plan before the Club could even begin negotiations with the local Council, the Club **must** have known it was in trouble, because thereafter, every time someone at the Club even seemed to suggest a new site, the local residents created such a fuss that the Club was forced to abandon each proposal. Many fans argued that the only edifices that appeared to be built in or around Maidstone, without so much as a whimper from local residents, appeared to be large hyper- and super-markets!

For many fans at the time though, the most interesting part of the brochure, were the financial figures:-

Net proceeds from the
sale of the London Road ground =   £2,833,000

Overdraft at the time of the sale =   370,031
Purchase of a house within the ground =   116,900
Greyhound Lease purchase =   400,000
Legal & Professional fees =   119,440

Dartford Ground improvements
A) Initial to 31.5.89   =   53,349
B) Football League to 30.9.90 =   464,930
Trading loss for 1988/89   =   262,265

                                           £1,786,915

Subtract £1,786,915 from £2,833,000 and we are left with the sum of £1,046,085, minus the Football League 'entry fee' of £200,000, and the Club were left with £846,085. From this figure, Maidstone United had annual rent obligations to the following:-

Bowerdene House =   £16,000
Anchorians   =   2,160
London Road =   3,500
Leafy Lane   =   690
Corinthians =   8,500
Dartford   =   35,000

                         £65,850

Subtract £65,850 from £846,085 and a figure of £780,235 is left. Presumably from this amount, the Club had electricity and heating bills, rates, players and staff wages, miscellaneous matchday costs and a myriad of other bills. It was clear to see that unless the Stones packed them in week after week, and that the lottery made huge amounts, then the Club was in trouble.

> The list as detailed in the Brochure.

THE 49 SITES WE HAVE CONSIDERED

1. Woodcut Farm (Ashford Road, Hollingbourne)
2. Hermitage Lane (South East of Barming Station, Aylesford)
3. Hermitage Lane (North West of Barming Station, Aylesford)
4. Hermitage Lane (opposite Hospital, Maidstone)
5. Bunyards Farm (London Road, Aylesford)
6. Allington Quarry (London Road, Aylesford)
7. North of Cobtree Park, (Bluebell Hill, Aylesford)
8. Culand Pit (Burham)
9. Beulah Wood (Sittingbourne Road, Boxley Parish)
10. County Showground (Detling)
11. Newnham Court Farm (Bearsted Road, Boxley (west side))
12. Newnham Court Farm (Bearsted Road, Boxley (east side))
13. Gidds Pond Farm (Bearsted Road, Boxley)
14. Langley Park Farm (Sutton Road, Boughton Monchelsea)
15. Sutton Road (Parkwood, Maidstone/Otham)
16. Brishing Lane (Boughton Monchelsea)
17. Walnut Tree Farm (Tovil)
18. Allotment site (Sandling Road, Maidstone)
19. West Malling Airfield
20. 20/20 Industrial Site
21. Rowe Place Farm (Aylesford)
22. Pratling Street
23. Sandell Perkins
24. Aylesford Sports Field
25. Sandhole, Snodland
26. Cornwallis Estate (Linton Crossroads)
27. West bank of River Medway (opposite Springfield)
28. Crossington Fields (top of Bluebell Hill)
29. The 100 Acre Field Allington (corner of Hermitage Lane and A20)
30. The ''D'' Field Allington (facing A20 Roundabout)
31. The Preston Hall Hospital, Ditton
32. The Leybourne Grange Estate
33. Land at top of Bluebell Hill owned by Sterling Homes
34. Cobtree Park
35. North of Horish Wood, Detling Village, owned by H Batchellor
36. Eccles Village, Sports Field owned by Blue Circle Cement
37. Birling Ashes A20/A228 (green belt)
38. Leybourne Lakes
39. Fire Brigade site, Linton
40. Rear of Police Headquarters, Parkwood
41. Harbourland, Boxley
42. Army Barracks, Sandling Road
43. Boarley Farm, Boxley
44. Reeds, Larkfield
45. Mote Park
46. Hermitage Farm
47. The Hermitage, West Malling
48. Hermitage Lane (north of Hospital, Maidstone)
49. Snodland (east of A228)

Many fans were shocked to see the amount which Dartford F.C. charged, especially in light of the amount of money spent on improving the ground. What was puzzling though was the costs on Leafy Lane, which is adjacent to the London Road training ground and what exactly did Maidstone United use Anchorians for? None of this was ever made clear, and they seemed that for a Club in financial trouble, as the Stones clearly were, to be extravagances that could not be afforded.

The next question that the brochure tried to address, was what had been done to find a new site suitable for a stadium. In the centre of the brochure was a reproduction of the Ordnance Survey map for Maidstone, with 49 markers, which represented every site proposed by the planning committee and apparently considered by the Club. At first glance, this appeared to represent the Club in a good light, they had obviously been 'hard at it'. Or had they? Few of the sites were worth serious consideration, and some were just farcical! Number 33 is described as 'Land at the top of Bluebell Hill owned by Sterling homes'. Bluebell Hill is a local beauty spot, with a panoramic view of Maidstone, Aylesford and beyond. No one would ever consider the site remotely suitable for a football stadium, and the access was nowhere near that required. Three sites were starred: Number 1 was the site at Woodcut Farm, Hollingbourne, about 7 miles from Maidstone, whilst 2 and 3 were South-east and North-west of Barming Station. The latter two were the favourites as far as the supporters and most observers were concerned, but it was Number 1 that would become the focus for all of the attention later on.

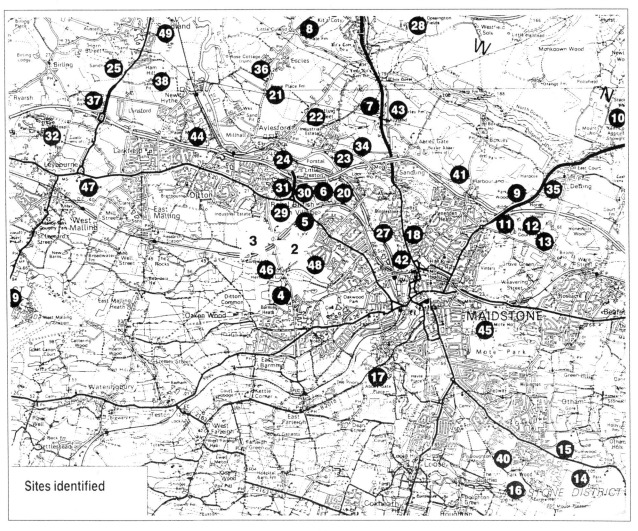

Sites identified

If anything was clear from that first brochure, it was the fact that the Club would need financial backing for any scheme that they put forward. This they apparently had, as on the inside back cover were a list of blue chip companies who had apparently formed a consortium and would finance any project. These included Whitbread Developments Ltd, GJW Government relations, The Principals group and more. A few wondered exactly what these companies wanted in return, we would soon find out via a second brochure that was released, giving details of not only a football stadium, but a sports and leisure complex on a grand scale.

Quite what Jim Thompson thought would be achieved by the first brochure is difficult to see, however the reaction cannot have been planned. Most supporters simply didn't believe most of what was in it and felt that the Club was only telling their side of the story in some sort of public relations exercise. The word 'whitewash' sprang to many minds. What was clear to see, was that Maidstone United would have great difficulty in ever returning to the County Town to a new stadium, unless someone else paid for it. It could be interpreted that the Chairman authorised the brochure's publication simply to head off the growing criticisms that the Club never issued any information. 'What is going on', became an almost constant bleat from the fans. Only an indecently short period of time had passed before another brochure was published, this one was to have a far greater impact.

The Club made an important, but subtle change in the second brochure, placing a photograph of a young fan on the front cover, with a light grey photograph of the Stone's open top bus ride subtly placed in the background. At the bottom of the front cover were the words, *"A Plea for a Sporting Change"*. This brochure was **not** aimed at the supporters. It was aimed at the heart of Commercial Maidstone. The title of the brochure was directed not to install fervour from the fans, but approached the public in a much more subtle way. Inside there was a very brief, and expurgated version of the history of the club. The emphasis was placed on the fact that the original purpose of the Athletic Ground on the London Road was to provide a multi (sporting) purpose facility. It also stated that Maidstone United had attempted to revive this concept in the 1970's with the introduction of Squash, Rugby League, and Greyhound racing.

The 'blurb' went on to explain that despite that despite their gallant efforts, the ground had: a) deteriorated too much, and b) that the urban expansion of suburbia surrounding the ground, prevented the development of the one thing that the Club didn't have room to provide - a car park. It is ironic that when the club eventually got to a planning application meeting, one Councillor objected saying that he would not vote for any plan with a car park included!

The text went on to explain that the sale of the ground was in fact just the first step in Maidstone United's chivalrous attempt to provide the town with the sort of complex that, *"the citizen of 21st century Maidstone will enjoy, equal to those provided for their Victorian ancestors."*

The brochure, adorned with pleasant pastel coloured designs, maps and diagrams, attempted to explain how the club had spent considerable time and effort in choosing what they felt was the best site for their plans. The site was some 4½ miles or so outside of Maidstone Town centre at Woodcut Farm near Hollingbourne. In actual fact, the Maidstone Borough Council had already refused a previous application to build a ground on the site, thus cynics might have suggested that the site was the **least** suitable so far as football was concerned. However, the Club supported this plan with details of how the traffic situation was ideal, how the effect of what they planned would not adversely disturb the local residents - the nearest of which was situated about 300 yards away - and how the town of Maidstone, and indeed, Kent would benefit from the complex. For Complex it was.

Finance had been promised by a group, which included several very large companies, who had obviously seen the financial benefits of such a plan. In addition to a 10,000 seater soccer stadium, there was to be full size artificial training pitches which would be used for hockey, football training and several other sports. There would also be an additional full size grass pitch, international standard athletics facilities for running, throwing and jumping, a 2km jogging trail, 32 lane bowling alley, health and fitness centre, remedial sports injury clinic, storage facilities for all local football Leagues and sports users of the complex, a budget hotel, a community social facility, 10 plex cinema, theme restaurants, a suite of dedicated committee and conference rooms, function suites and discotheque, new B.R. Station with 200 parking spaces, a park-and-ride base (with parking for 2000 cars), and a new site for the Maidstone cattle market.

Even to the least cynical of supporters, once one had waded through the rhetoric and 'blurb', the actual concept was quite incredible. The town of Maidstone, apart from being the County town of Kent, is basically a centre of commerce, and prides itself as being such. The problem was, and indeed is, that people live there too. For several years the Council has been aware that as far as leisure-time facilities are concerned, Maidstone really has very little to offer. Therefore, most felt that such an ambitious and innovative complex, that was to be provided **not** from their tax or rates would be welcomed. Sadly, most people don't count. The promise was made by Jeremy Hindle, nearly two and half years previously, at the Conference Championship civic reception, which ran: *"You're the ones who have done it and now Maidstone's got to provide something for you hasn't it? and I give you this promise, we will do our level best to find whatever we can for you. That's right and proper for you now."*

The majority of Maidstone fans remembered those words, and hopeful anticipation had turned into cynical resentment and bitterness. The Council had done very little to help the club, in fact every time that the Club announced interest in one site or another, the 'NIMBY' lobby had appeared, and the Council had stated that the Club should look elsewhere. But here was a new and exciting project that everyone should want, surely even the NIMBY's would applaud this proposal which would benefit the town and area? The fans were to be bitterly disappointed.

The proposed new stadium

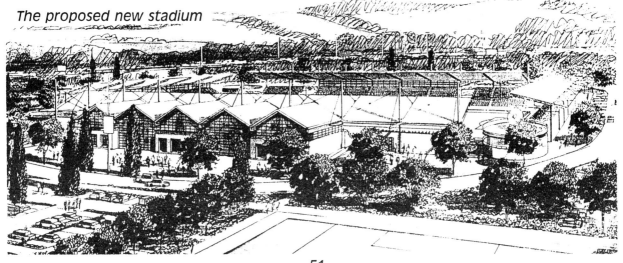

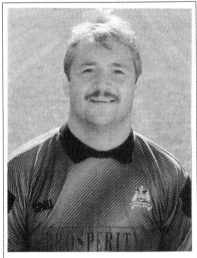

In - Iain Hesford

Out - Gary Cooper

Following the issue of the two brochures, and the predictable howls of protest from local residents, Maidstone United's team had to prepare for 1992/93. Graham Carr and the team, somewhat sensibly, attempted to ignore the furore concerning the Club's future and concentrate on playing the game. There were several new additions to the squad, notably ex-Gillingham Captain - Paul Haylock, Robbie Painter, Liberd Henry, plus Iain Hesford, a goalkeeper purchased on the cheap from Hull City. Mark Beeney had been sold to Brighton and Mark Gall would follow before the end of the season. Ken Charlery and Gary Cooper had gone to Peterborough in a joint deal, whilst Steve Butler was by this time, playing for Watford.

The sales of these players upset the supporters, not because they were nearly all sold at knock down prices, but because the fans felt that without them, Maidstone United would have to build up a new squad from scratch. Maidstone fans had never been noted for their patience, and this was no exception! As it turned out, Mark 'Smokey' Gall would be an almost instant hit at Brighton, scoring several great goals and dazzling defenders with his electrifying pace. Gall, together with Kenny Charlery, and Warren Barton at Wimbledon, would all be voted 'Player of the year' by supporters at their respective clubs after just one season. It therefore appears strange that someone like Graham Carr, who boasted a pedigree as a Manager, failed to see the potential that he had at the club. It is no surprise either that none of the players sold by Graham Carr had any of the physical attributes of his ideal footballer.

The 'new' Stones, a squad that Graham Carr had formed, contained only a few familiar names. Jason Lillis and Gary Stebbing were still with the Club as was Darren Oxbrow and Paul Rumble. Dave Madden and Nicky Johns, both reported as injured, were never to play during the season, and towards the end, the latter announced his retirement from the game.

The season began badly, with successive 3-0 defeats away at Chesterfield in the League and Leicester City in the first leg of the League Cup. The first home match of the season, against

Halifax, also saw a dismal defeat, by 1-0. Leicester City then arrived for the second leg of the League Cup and although the Stones played well, Leicester snatched a vital goal to ease them through to the next round. The Stones then travelled to Aldershot, who had themselves survived attempts to close the Club, but were still seriously in debt, and would disappear before the season's end. In debt they may have been, but on the field, they showed they could play, tearing Maidstone apart and easily winning 3-0. It appeared that this was more than enough for the Manager and the Club announced his resignation the following day.

The Supporters were jubilant. They had been very unhappy with Graham Carr from the start, and even Jim Thompson in a letter to the writer, had described his style as 'abrasive'. Carr had more or less stopped all forms of communication with anyone. A conversation with Mike Evans, the programme Editor the previous season, revealed that not only had he and Graham Carr violently disagreed several times, but that the Manager had on more than one occasion, either forgotten or refused to hand him any 'copy' for his column in the programme, and Mike had ended up 'ghost writing' the column himself! More often than not, whenever the manager appeared from the tunnel a chorus of, *"Carr out",* from the fans on the terraces would go up. Whilst most officials dismissed this as ignorance, the writer's attitude is that whilst the fans may not always understand the intricate technicalities of the game, they **do** know what they like! The style of football which Graham Carr had tried to impose on the team, was totally alien to the supporters, who had been bought up on a diet of high scoring, flowing open football.

The best way to describe Graham Carr's style was with the three 'D' words, 'Dour, Depressing and Dreadful'! To be fair to Graham Carr, he appreciated that what he needed to do was to get the team winning. It was just his methods that no one liked. However, it is certain had the team performed well for him, then he would have been hailed as a hero. Such is the fickleness of supporters.

The Club toyed with the idea of advertising for a new Manager, but appointed Bill Williams, the General Manager to the post. It would mean that Bill had been in charge of the team at three different times! Clive Walker, Graham Carr's assistant, would remain as the team coach. The first match with them in charge, bought Maidstone's first points, a 1-1 home draw against Cardiff City, however this was followed by an away defeat at Scunthorpe, a surprising, but welcome 2-1 victory at home to Walsall, before a poor 2-0 defeat at home to Lincoln City. Bill Williams was very much of the old school, and he made it known that he was trying to install some pride in the players. The first time this showed was at Rotherham, where the team 'dug deep' and fought for a tremendous 3-3 draw. This was to be Mark Gall's last game for the Stones before he was sold to Brighton.

This draw was followed by a 1-0 victory over York City, a 'shock' 2-1 defeat against non-League Landlords, Dartford, in the Kent Senior Cup, and a 2-0 defeat at Mansfield. Consistency was a problem, and when the Stones could get any points, invariably it was just the one gained from a battling draw. However, there were signs that the team was beginning to gel, for although defeats were regular, some of the performances were very good. Iain Hesford proved himself to be a big hit with the fans, he even scored a goal against Hereford!

Whilst Bill Williams and Clive Walker were struggling to get the team going, off the field developments were taking place as regards the proposed sports complex. Jim Thompson assured the supporters that the Council were being very co-operative, however, several

Councillors began to air their objections. The hearing for the application had been set for Monday November 11th 1992, at the Town's corn exchange. It had originally been planned to use the Town Hall, but as the local interest in the application was so great, the Council switched it.

Before the application could be heard however, there was a great deal of canvassing around the borough. It almost seemed as if it was an election, with those for and against distributing leaflets and taking out full page newspaper advertisements to further their cause. Maidstone United sent the scale model 'on tour' to various locations, along with planning and development experts, to show people exactly what they were proposing. They claimed tremendous success, saying that most people asked had supported their bid. The local Kent Messenger ran a telephone poll, 5590 voted for the scheme with just 600 against. Those against it 'poo-pooed' the result, saying that supporters could have phoned as many times as they wished to boost the numbers. Then, just before the meeting was due to take place, Michael Heseltine - the Environment Secretary - stepped in to place a holding order on the scheme. This meant that even if the Council voted for the scheme, it would have to be referred to Mr Heseltine. This was a blow to the Club, but by then it was clear to most people, that Jim Thompson's confidence was sadly awry, and most of the Labour councillors stated they would stand against the scheme.

Early on the Monday evening, those Maidstone supporters who could, left their work places early to turn up at the Corn Exchange, all of them bedecked in yellow and black. There were banners, *"Bring the Stones home"*, *"Please vote yes"*, and even one that said, *"fulfil your promise"*. The problem was that the hall only held around 270 people, and nearly 1,800 turned up. There was an outward air of joviality amongst the supporters, although on each and every face there was evidence of tension, evidence that this could be the greatest night of the Stone's life.....or the worst. Inside the hall, everyone quickly identified the small group of NIMBY's - there were no more than 10! How brave they were to be present!

Outside the hall, there was a sizeable group of around 1,500 fans, all chanting and singing happily. The first speeches began, and it was soon obvious to everyone whether the speaker was either for or against the plan. Those who supported the scheme were vociferously cheered, those who opposed it were booed, hissed and jeered. It also became fairly obvious early on, that there were only two or three Councillors supporting the application, and opposed by Mark Watts and Wendy Marlowe at the vanguard of the Labour group within the Council. Jim Thompson was summoned to speak, and began with the line, *"I've been in charge of Maidstone United for twenty years and have been given five minutes in which to save it"*. He argued that the Council's planning report was flawed and that it had not taken everything into consideration. He warned that should the application be rejected, the Club would be forced into liquidation almost immediately. As he left the stand, the supporters gave a long standing ovation. Jim Thompson had always been a very convincing orator.

Mark Watts, one of the 'new breed' of Labour politicians, began with the words, *"I have a dream"*, to which a wag shouted, *"Wake up then"*, which sent a guffaw around the hall. Watts then began an argument against the application, which essentially stated that he refused to vote for anything which included a car park. To the writer, this appears to be an intriguing standpoint, and one which is still maintained. If so, then there must be many applications refused by this man. The next up was Wendy Marlowe. She was another Labour Councillor, more in the mould of a left-wing Mary Whitehouse than a potential Barbara Castle.

She claimed that prior to the planning meeting, she had received threats and abusive phone calls. The whole thing was becoming petty and unbelievable, at least to those of us who were football fans. As such, supporters are easy to accuse of such outrageous actions, albeit that this is largely their own fault. Even if these allegations were true, the fact that it had been revealed two days before in the newspaper, showed that she wished it to be considered as an influencing argument. This in fact was just the latest in a string of ridiculous and totally fabricated stories that were levelled at the Maidstone fans.

The Stone's supporters had been accused, during the 'campaigning', of being the worst of the worst hooligans around. According to various anti-complex sources, Maidstone fans terrorised the local inhabitants of Dartford whenever their team was playing at Watling Street, with every act of vandalism from throwing bricks and bottles through people's windows to urinating in their front gardens! Those whose vivid imaginations concocted these stories are the sort who probably believe all that is written about the behaviour of football supporters. Those that don't normally read the tabloid press, but are prepared to read and believe them when it suits.

This was the era of Margeret Thatcher and her campaign against football fans. It was obvious that many of the Tory voters were more than ready to jump on the Thatcher anti-football bandwagon, inventing stories that 'were probably true'. The truth was that Maidstone United had trouble even attracting supporters to the ground, let alone enough to cultivate a gang of thugs in their midst. There **had** been the occasional 'skirmish' at a Stone's match but usually there were hardly a large enough number of spectators at a game to cause any real 'aggro'. Whilst Maidstone United could never really have claimed that their matches had a family atmosphere the fans had never 'boasted' a hooligan core. Obviously most Maidstone fans didn't believe Mrs Marlow's claims, although she insists to this day that they did happen.

Of course the application was rejected, by some 10 votes to 2, the Liberal Democrats, abstaining and thus allowing the application to fail. Outside the hall, there were tears, and chants of *"What's it like to kill a club"*, whilst Jim Thompson was mobbed and urged to continue the club. For a few moments, a group of around 200 fans faced six or seven policemen, with the thought of hunting down a few of the Councillors as they left. Fortunately, the moment passed and the fans dispersed.

The next day, the Club announced that it would have to seriously consider voluntary liquidation, that it was losing £1,500 a day and really had no choice. The Club was supposed to play Sutton United in the F.A.Cup the following Saturday, and the news was shattering to most fans. It now appeared that there was absolutely no money left from the £2.8 million, some asked angrily, where had it all gone?

In the event, Jim Thompson changed his mind and vowed to keep fighting, saying, *"My advice is that not only we will win the appeal, we shall also gain costs from the Council. We are not going to lie down and let them get away with this"*. He criticised the Council Planning Committee, with some justification, it has to be said, of being shortsighted and more interested in petty inter-party politics than making decisions that would benefit the whole community. These claims were of course strenuously denied by the Council. Maidstone United would carry on, as much in defiance of the Planning Committee's decision as anything else. In fact, they completed their League season.

STONE DEAD?

THE decision to throw out Maidstone United's plan provoked angry scenes outside the Corn Exchange last night.

Staff and supporters of the Fourth Division club, many of whom were unable to get in to hear the debate, showed their emotions following an overwhelming decision to reject the stadium and leisure proposal at Woodcut Farm, Hollingbourne.

Members of the planning and transportation committee voted 11-2 against the £30 million application on the grounds that it was against the council's rural planning policies.

Interestingly, the man who masterminded the whole project, club chairman Jim Thompson, was not present to see his plans scuppered.

He had already left the stormy meeting which, at times, had threatened to degenerate as passions reached boiling point.

Councillors had to speak against a background of noise and committee chairman Cllr Helen Drummond had on several occasions to call for calm.

Around 260 people filled the

They duly beat Sutton United 1-0, but made hard work of it. Both Jim Thompson and the Club appealed for more supporters to turn up at Watling Street to show solidarity. It may have worked in Poland, but at Watling Street, there was little discernable difference to the gates. Even Burnley, who bought nearly 2000 supporters with them and were even given the complete length of the covered terracing, could only boost the attendance to 2,375!

With the Club in serious financial trouble, saviours were many and varied. Brian Talbot, the ex-Arsenal, Ipswich and England player arrived on the scene around February, complete with partner, and entrepreneur, Mark English. There was talk of a possible takeover by the pair. They watched Maidstone United beat Carlisle 5-1 and a superb hat-trick by Bradley Sandeman. They also turned up for another couple of matches, and the local media reported that they were 'in discussion' with the Club. In effect this meant with Jim Thompson, he was after all the major shareholder.

On the field, the team, under the guidance of Bill Williams, were looking better, but still not consistent enough. After the spanking of Carlisle, followed a 3-2 defeat away at Barnet and a humiliating 4-2 loss at Wrexham. The team hovered around the 18th or 19th spot in the League, not at the bottom, if only because the form of teams such as York, Halifax and Doncaster Rovers, was even worse than the Stones.

The end of the season arrived with a spate of draws, the last game being away at Doncaster Rovers. Little were the Maidstone fans to know it would turn out to be the last match Maidstone United ever played. The matchday programme for that match was to increase so much in value that within just three months, collectors were asking £10 for a copy!

STONES BOSS STEPS DOWN

English is new MD but Thompson will stay on

By MARK BRISTOW

MAIDSTONE United chairman Jim Thompson handed control of the club over to property investor Mark English after seven hours of talks yesterday.

On the day that the club officially lodged its appeal over a proposed new stadium at Woodcut Farm, Hollingbourne, 27-year-old Mr English was installed as the club's managing director.

The move which coincides with an injection of £800,000 of Mr English's funds, also brings to an end Mr Thompson's 20 years in control of the club.

While he will remain on the board as chairman but his majority shareholding will be transferred to Mr English who will head all future policy making decisions.

Jim Thompson: handing over control of Stones

holder, declined to talk about the appeal.

Borough planner and surveyor Trevor Gasson said the council would be insisting on a public inquiry because of the high public profile of the issue.

Mr English originally appeared on the scene in February after responding to national newspaper advertisements which put the club up for sale at £300,000.

The end of the 1991/92 season finished at Doncaster, and for most fans, it was time to turn their full attention to the plight of the Club. It was clear that the Club was in Financial trouble, although the sum was, in football terms, a pittance - about £800,000. Aldershot had already suffered liquidation, which left Northampton Town, Halifax, Brighton and of course, the Stones, appearing to be jostling in their efforts **not** to be the next Club to go down. In 1991, an advertisement had appeared in the Financial Times, offering for sale a Fourth Division football Club. Jim Thompson denied it was the Stones.

Most fans felt that the lack of money was easily curable. One often heard of takeovers, surely someone with some money would come in? Then at the start of May 1992, the Kent Messenger announced that Maidstone United had indeed been saved. Mark English, had purchased control of the Club from Jim Thompson, and would be leading them forward from then on. Thompson would remain as a member of the board, but Mark English would, for all intents and purposes, be the new boss. The reaction of the fans was euphoric. The team had shown some promise, some potential towards the end of the 1990/91 season, and now that could be built on to restart the Club's rise up the Football League. Personally, the writer felt happy about the situation, for Brian Talbot and Mark English had been spoken to earlier after an evening match, and they had asked various questions about how some of the fans felt. Brian Talbot was already a vague acquaintance for he had been the guest of honour at the awards ceremony at the end of season dinner when the writer had been working alongside Steve Birley at Elmore A.F.C. in Tiverton, Devon.

What would the fans think of a proposal to groundshare with Gillingham? What was the likely potential crowds? They scoffed when it was suggested that the majority of fans would accept such a plan, if only because Gillingham was nearer than Dartford (although in retrospect it could be argued that a few 'diehards' would have seen such a move as a 'sell out'). The writer caused some amusement by predicting that Maidstone United could have expected an average gate of around 3,500 - 4,000 if their future were secure, and they played nearer - if not actually in Maidstone. Whilst these sort of gates had never been achieved on a regular basis by Maidstone United at any time there is good reason to suppose such figures as reasonable. There were many football fans in Maidstone who had never seen United play, many who had refused to travel to Dartford, yet when Maidstone played Gillingham they came out in their droves. One reason was no doubt the fact that Priestfield is nearer and easier to get to than Watling Street. And of course there is the 'Gillingham' factor. It was well known that many Gill's fans watched Maidstone United, when their team were away (although they might not admit to it!), therefore a sizeable crowd from the local area would not have been unreasonable.

Fresh crisis as new boss quits Stones

MAIDSTONE United was facing a fresh crisis this week when managing director Mark English quit less than a week after assuming the role.

The 27-year-old property investor said he had not appreciated the severity of the club's financial problems.

He said the directors had forced his hand after he proposed that the club went into receivership, although he had no quarrel with Jim Thompson who had remained supportive.

Mr English's departure leaves Maidstone continuing to look for a benefactor as it fights against rising debts, estimated at more than £600,000, including daily losses of £1,500.

Jim Thompson, whose hands were thrust back into the reigns with Mr English's departure, was reluctant to go into detail about what caused the resignation.

But one of the directors on the board, who did not wish to be named, said: "Mr English said he had not been aware of how serious the debts of the club were. But as far as I know he

Reign ends after week 'due to the extent of club debts'

But, just when we thought that the Club was back on the rails, the whole thing collapsed yet again. Within days, Mark English had 'resigned' from the Club. In his statement, he cited, *"previously Unknown debts"*, as the reason. However, the truth was the fact that he didn't have the money to begin with. Many voiced the opinion that he was little more than a con-man, who had already tried it on with Aldershot. One wonders, with that in mind, why Jim Thompson had even agreed to talk to him. Mark English was, supposedly, a property investor, who had, according to his own admission, made some £2.8 million. He was a majority shareholder in Kettering Town - the GM Vauxhall Conference Club - and to all intents and purposes, a suitable candidate, and able to purchase the Club.

Several months after the affair, a Sunday tabloid newspaper ran an exposè on Mark English and his dealings. He had been involved in another similar 'takeover' bid at Aldershot, and had been refused entrance to his executive box at 'Spurs for non-payment, before turning his attention to Maidstone United. The Kent Messenger also revealed the details of his dealings with Jim Thompson. Mr English had, it seems, indicated that an £800,000 long term loan would be injected into the Stones, on top of the purchasing fee. In return, Mark English would receive £200,000 paid into one of his companies. According to Jim Thompson, English also agreed to fund the Club's appeal against the complex planning decision, which was estimated would cost about £200,000. But Jim Thompson demanded an initial guarantee of £50,000, which would be used to pay some of the more urgent and immediate bills, and to ensure that long overdue wage bills and other payments were settled within a week. As an act of good faith, Maidstone United paid £7,500 from their bank account into a bank account in Kettering. The Club were informed that this new account had an already arranged facility for a £200,000 overdraft.

However, things began to look odd, when salary payments were not honoured, and upon further investigation the bank account in Kettering had not received the mandate for the payments. Jim Thompson then got all the staff to check their own salary cheques, only to find that they had all been returned marked, *"refer to drawer"*. Mr Thompson demanded an explanation from Mark English and according to the former, *"he stood here in this office, in front of his accountant, and handed me a Cheque... I took it to Dartford and arranged that they should immediately ring the bank and clear the cheque......by the time I got back to Maidstone, it had been stopped"*. Later, it was revealed that Mark English had also paid for a meal on the Club's account, had stopped the cheque for £50,000, and had even drawn money on the Club account **after** he had left!

Later, Jim Thompson said that he had seen documentation to the effect that the Allied Dunbar bank in London would be loaning £2.1 million to Mark English and that he was represented by a very respectable firm of solicitors. Mark English, under some pressure, duly resigned at a board meeting on May 18th 1992. The saviour of Maidstone United had lasted less than a week! English later resigned from Kettering Town, again after some ignominious goings on, and his whereabouts since then are unknown. Taking into consideration that Jim Thompson supposedly is a corporate businessman, it is difficult to understand why £7,500 was paid to Mark English as a sign of good faith. Surely, the sign of good faith should have been received **from** Mr English? Perhaps, as had been suggested amongst the fans, the Chairman was so desperate that he was prepared to have done anything to save the club, even to the point of apparently giving money away!

Following the collapse of this takeover, the future of the Club was once again plunged into doubt. Creditors, sensing perhaps that this was the end, appeared from all quarters. For most fans, the whole saga was unreal. Surely a Football League Club wouldn't go out of business for just £800,000, not when transfers at Premier League level were nearer the £2½ million mark? Surely there was someone with money who cared? Certainly the writer did, and at the time as Chairman of the Kent Branch of the Football Supporters Association - although the branch numbered only a handful of active members, the majority of them from Gillingham - something had to be done, however ineffectual.

The GOAL! exhibition at Wembley, where the F.S.A. had a stand, was visited. To be frank, the exhibition was a farce, and despite the fact that Leicester City were playing Blackburn in the Division 2 play-offs that afternoon, the number of supporters and trade stands that attended the show was pitiful. Undeterred, a petition was started with supporters at the show, showing that people from all over the country really cared about Maidstone United. In the end around 3,000 signatures were obtained from supporters from as far afield as Scotland, Holland and even one from the U.S.A.! No one who was asked refused, with the notable exception of Geoff Hurst, the England 'Hero' from 1966. He more or less said he couldn't care less. In retrospect perhaps, it might have been better trying in Maidstone itself, but it was important for the Club to know that the popular image of parochially minded football supporters, who were interested only in their own team, was wrong and they **did** care about football in general.

On the Monday morning after the show, the Club offices were visited in the hope of presenting the petition to Jim Thompson. There was a TV camera crew present as well as the local newspaper man, and they filmed the writer handing over the petition to Jim Thompson, who also looked bemused. He

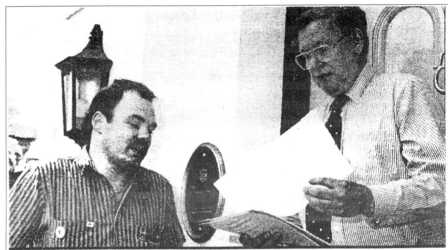

Maidstone chairman Jim Thompson inspects the petition handed to him by Mike George, chairman of the Kent branch of the Football Supporters' Association, at the club's headquarters

was also somewhat irritated, justifiably so. *"What am I supposed to do with that?"* he asked. A somewhat mumbled answer suggested he read it and that he ought to know that there were lots of people who didn't want to see the Stones go down. I suddenly felt that it was a pointless exercise. Jim Thompson was right. What **was** he supposed to do with it? What did it really signify? There was annoyance with the media, for although they had not tricked the writer - they had explained what they wanted to do - but on hindsight their request to hand it over in front of their cameras should have been refused, since the whole thing looked tacky on the evening news. No wonder Jim Thompson was irritated!

The crises with the Club, now centred upon Bowerdene House, the Club's Maidstone offices. Supporters would phone the staff attempting to find out information, however there was little they could say. Rumours abounded, for it had been made public that Jim Thompson had purchased shares in Dartford Football Club, who of course were the Stone's landlords. In one way, this was a shrewd business move, it meant that Dartford became part of Jim Thompson's empire and would therefore be able to drop their rent. However, the 'Darts' were in as much financial difficulty as Maidstone, therefore there was a crises there as well. Rumours began to emerge (although they would not be finally confirmed publicly until much later when the Kent Messenger published a special 'investigative' report into the Club's downfall), that things were very amiss at the Club. To the supporters, the writer included, this was all very confusing. There was mention of the companies 'North Kent Holdings Ltd' and 'Harvest Publications Ltd', which, at the time, meant very little.

It emerged that Jim Thompson not only controlled these companies, but that bits and pieces of Maidstone United Football Club Ltd were effectively owned by them. Jim Thompson's wife and relatives held key positions and shares as well. It appeared that this state of affairs dated back to the 1980's and the 'boardroom takeover'. By issuing extra shares to his wife and relatives, Jim Thompson ensured with this piece of 'corporate nepotism', that no such occurrence would ever repeat itself! Maidstone United therefore was not only apparently penniless, but extremely fragmented to boot.

End of era as Stones call in liquidators

by MARK BRISTOW

AN ANNOUNCEMENT was hardly necessary when Jim Thompson and his directors emerged on Monday with the news that the club would be going into liquidation.

The message was etched on their faces and for one fleeting moment the harsh reality of Maidstone's situation was there for all to see.

All the toils, the endless planning meetings, the lobbying and impassioned wrangling were at an end. Maidstone United, as a Barclays League side at least, were being laid to rest.

It was an emotional moment as Mr Thompson moved to share his anguish with those who had been most loyal to the Maidstone cause.

From the man who guided Maidstone to the pinnacle of non-league soccer and into the Barclays League the trump cards were now exhausted. For the first time since assuming the chair in 1970 Mr Thompson was forced to admit defeat.

"It was all about sacrifices," he lamented. "We made sacrifices, Maidstone council didn't. That's what killed the club.

Demolition of Stones' London Road ground — the site was bought by furnishing company MFI

guess it's inevitable that the old chestnut of the London Road ground will come up and how it was a mistake to leave there.

"But it was always a move which we had to make — the bank insisted on it and we made sure that we planned our strategy quite carefully.

"As far as we were concerned Maidstone United would be moving into one of the finest new stadiums in the country on the Hollingbourne site.

Mr Thompson added: "Trevor Gasson (Borough Planning Officer and Surveyor) admitted in originally pointing out the site that there

resource as well to our application.

"If we had gone straight to appeal that time then money would not have been wasted and the club would at this moment in time still have been safe."

He went on to: "It is the supporters and in particular the young people

groundsharing with Beazer Homes League Dartford at Watling Street had also helped to accelerate the club's slide.

"That was also the crunch," admitted Mr Thompson. "Having the lowest gates in the Fourth Division didn't help our cause.

"But compared with other groundsharers such as Wimbledon (at Crystal Palace) and Chester (at Macclesfield) our gates did not fall that dramatically as a percentage.

"That is why I think that Hollingbourne could have been such a tremendous success. Our supporters would have been accommodated in one of the finest stadiums in the country and would have benefited from all of the other facilities which would have been provided."

Mr Thompson declared that it was his intention to be a part of any future schemes and added that he would continue to preside over the plans to site a multi-purpose leisure and stadium complex at Hollingbourne, which were now with the Department of the Environment for appeal consideration.

In the meantime he faces a fresh battle to preserve his place on the FA Council where he is the representative for the Division 10 region which takes in Kent, East Sussex and part of Essex.

"I will now be able to devote

In June, Jim Thompson announced that the Club would be going into voluntary liquidation. Again he blamed the local Council, saying that whilst he and Maidstone United had made sacrifices, the Council had not. The meeting to officially wind the Club up, was set for June 17th. Shareholders and creditors would be there to finalise the details. But, as the media waited for the announcement that the proverbial axe had fallen, Melvyn Rose, the appointed liquidator surprised everyone by stating that a mystery investor had come in at the '11th hour'. The formal announcement of the liquidation was put on hold. Maidstone fans held their breath.......they had already seen one 'saviour' leave.

The mystery man behind the late bid, was John Waugh, a prominent property developer from the North-east. Most fans had been vaguely aware that Jim Thompson had returned to his native Newcastle, though most thought he was visiting relatives and taking himself out of the spotlight for a while. John Waugh's proposals included the purchase of all the shares from Mr Thompson, the refinancing of the Club, and the paying off of all creditors. It certainly sounded good and John Waugh's credentials looked good. He had helped Sir John Hall to takeover Newcastle United and had only recently attempted to take over Berwick Rangers.

Bizarre twist in Maidstone tale

By MARK BRISTOW

MAIDSTONE UNITED have been laid to rest. After three turbulent seasons it was revealed late on Friday that all attempts to re-finance the club in their present state had failed.

That, however, is not the end of it. For in the most bizarre develop-

He nevertheless remained adamant that "the Stones will rise again", and accompanying the statement announcing the sell-out was another detailing plans for a new Maidstone club.

Through a company called the Football in Maidstone Development Group, Mr Thompson, along with other club stalwarts, has pledged to bring soccer back to the town.

The statement revealed that

However, there had been a bizarre twist to the tale in that Waugh had wanted to take Berwick to Newcastle to play, and that, it seemed, was the plan for Maidstone United. Basically it involved relocating the Club to the North-east, renaming them, the Newcastle Browns, and playing at St James' Park, the home of Newcastle United.

The reaction from the fans was uproar, once again the writer was summoned by the local media for a reaction. As best can be recalled, a simple statement that the idea was 'laughable' and 'ridiculous' was given. Like most Maidstone United supporters, the idea simply couldn't be believed that such a farcical plan had even been proposed, let alone considered. It was now quite clear that Jim Thompson's 'holiday' in the North-east had come up with a meeting with John Waugh and this plan. The Newcastle Browns? Move the Club to the North East? It sounded very much as though whoever had thought this up had obviously been drinking too much of the region's famous brew!

Despite the apparent stupidity of the scheme, Maidstone United Football Club owed money to the Inland Revenue, Kent Police, employees of the club, playing staff, Customs and Excise, and more. In addition, Dartford Chairman, Bernie Rogers announced that Watling Street would be sold and that there were several interested parties. At least one thing was sure, Maidstone United had played their last match at Dartford. On 28 June, at a board meeting, Maidstone's board of Directors were told that only John Waugh's bid gave any chance that the Stones might be saved, therefore on August 4th, Jim Thompson sold his 150,000 shares for a nominal 1p a piece. After 22 years, Jim Thompson's dream had finally died. Most Maidstone supporters felt that their allegiance with Maidstone United also finished there and then. Jim Thompson, with whom the deal had obviously been done, had clearly turned his back on the fans and was apparently willing to let the Club go North. The fans could never forgive that. Although John Waugh's intentions were odd, to say the least, it was obvious that there was no way they could afford to travel to watch the team playing in the North-east, nor, to be quite frank, would they particularly wish to.

Almost immediately, John Waugh's proposals ran into trouble. Newcastle United declared that the only team sharing their stadium would be the Newcastle United reserves. Undaunted, they turned to Gateshead, hoping to lease the International stadium. This idea was also refused by Gateshead Council as 'inappropriate'. Perhaps most important of all the Football League stated that there was no chance that they would ratify such a plan, a fact that John

Waugh and Jim Thompson must have realised, although John Waugh was to later say that given more time, he could have 'persuaded' them. With the new season almost upon them, there was no indication as to whether Maidstone United would ever kick a ball or not. Most of the players were busy attempting to find new Clubs, they obviously didn't think there was much chance, whilst Scunthorpe United, Maidstone United's first opponents for the 1992-93 season, had to go ahead and print up copies of the matchday programme because they simply had no idea whether the Stones would honour the fixture or not. This programme immediately became a collector's item, for although the Club were unable to play the fixture, the programme had been produced, albeit with a blank space where the Maidstone United team should have been listed.

There was really no alternative open to John Waugh and his associates, other than to put the Club into Liquidation. This happened a day or so before the Scunthorpe match was due to be played on August 15th 1992. The Maidstone United story was finally over.

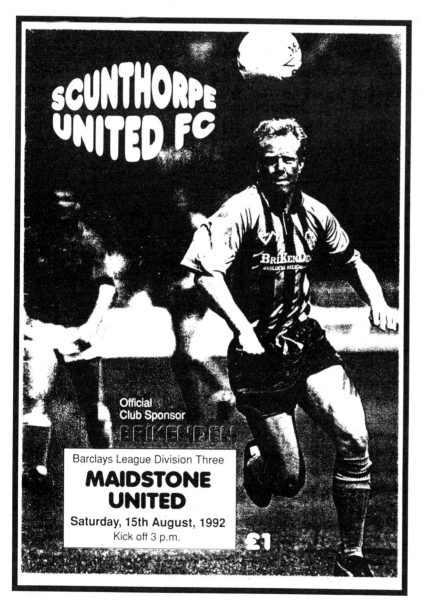

Scunthorpe United

1. Mark Samways
2. Joe Joyce
3. Paul Longden
4. Dave Hill
5. Matthew Elliott
6. Glenn Humphries
7. Dean Martin
8. Graham Alexander
9. Tony Daws
10. John Buckley
11. Ian Helliwell
12. Jason White
14. Andy Stevenson

Maidstone United

1.
2.
3.
4.
5.
6.
7.
8.
9.
10.
11.
12.
14.

CHAPTER 11

THE STONES INFLUENCE

Although Maidstone United never graced the 'hallowed turf' of Wembley, either as a non-League or Professional Club, there can be no doubt that they did have an influence on the world of football, both in and out of the League.

In terms of players, those that have worn the black and amber for the Stones, had they ever been accumulated in one team, could arguably have been a great side. Certainly within the realms of Kent and South-eastern Football, the Stones were an unparalleled success, even more so than their Football League neighbours, Gillingham. No other team had managed to accumulate so many trophies, or win those on offer with such frequency. It must remain a mystery why the Club never did better at a national level, the F.A. Vase and Trophy competitions were never a place where the Stones fared well. Even in terms of 'Giantkilling', the team didn't really capture the imaginations of the British public at large, despite having beaten Exeter City, Gillingham, and various others.

But, Maidstone was a fertile 'nursery' for talent, as can be seen by the list of those who have been through the Club on their way to greater success. The most obvious names are David Sadler (Manchester United & England), Warren Barton (Newcastle United & England Under 21), Mark Newson (Bournemouth & Fulham), Mark Beeney (Brighton & Leeds Utd), Steve Butler (Watford & Cambridge Utd), Kenny Charlery (Peterborough Utd) and Gary Cooper (Peterborough Utd & Birmingham City).

But apart from these honoured few, Maidstone also boasted many others and who are well known in non-League circles. Such names as John Bartley, Frank Ovard, Tony Lynch, Andy Woon, Steve Hamburger, Chris Kinnear, Dave Mehmet, Mark Golley, Tony Pamphlett, Dickie Guy, Peter Taylor, Brian Thompson and Mark Hill, are almost legendary names at this level, and many are now in Management.

As for Jim Thompson, if his contribution to the Club was immense, and it was, his contribution to the football world as a whole was also important. As Chairman of the Alliance Premier, Gola and later the GM Vauxhall Conference, he masterminded that League's development with clear ideas of where it needed to go. He recognised early on that the senior non-League Division needed credibility and needed to be recognised by the Professional Football League. As The Alliance League developed into the Gola League, there was a notable increase in interest as far as the Football League and advertisers were concerned. Jim Thompson was of course involved in the Stone's two abortive bids for Football League status, and realising perhaps that it would take more than just a couple of years success to make the Football League change their policies. He administered another change in the competition when it became the GM Vauxhall Conference and set about persuading the Football League to accept some form of automatic Promotion and relegation system. More than anyone else, Jim Thompson engineered the 'Pyramid' system with the chance for non-League Clubs to enter the Professional ranks.

As far as Maidstone United goes, it is probably fair comment to say that without Jim Thompson, the Club would never have got to the Football League. When he first arrived at the Club, that is what he promised the fans. It took him 20 years, but he delivered and fulfilled that promise. Jim Thompson was perhaps unusual in that he was essentially a businessman and Chairman, but on the whole more or less knew what he was talking about when the subject of football came up, especially it's development. Sadly, other events and influences bought an end to Jim Thompson and the Club, and there is evidence, many would claim, to suggest that Jim Thompson was not entirely without blame. However, no such blame should or can be laid wholly at his door. In many ways, he and the Club were the victims of circumstance, and the local Maidstone Borough Council, despite their denials, must carry a lot of responsibility for the Club's demise.

There is a school of thought, which suggests, and it is hard to refute, that had the council really **wanted** Maidstone United back in, or near the town, then they could and would have got them back, regardless of protest. But there are other factors to be considered as well. The population of Maidstone and the surrounding area must also shoulder a degree of the responsibility for the Club's demise. When the Club needed and indeed appealed for their support, it was ignored. It is sad when the townspeople simply do not care whether their senior football club exists or not, but in Maidstone's case, that is one of the major reasons why the Club folded. The people were asked, and begged to come and support the team. They, on the whole, ignored those pleas, despite being told that without their support, the Club would not survive. The people of Maidstone are by no means blameless for the Club's demise. It is difficult to believe that a senior Club, based in the town, will ever make much of an impression when faced with such seemingly inherent apathy. In that respect, the people of Maidstone neither want or deserve a senior football team. Other contributory factors must include the apparent and much publicised weakness of the Board at the Club. Many of the former Directors claim that they had little or no say in decisions, withe somewhat lame excuse that they were simply, *"following orders"*. Surely they cannot be saying that they simply did not have the collective courage to oppose any decisions with which they either didn't agree, or were not party too? Apparently they are.

Jim had a dream, and it was during the 1970's that the foundation for success was laid. The 1980's would prove to be the time when some of the seeds that had been sown burst into flower. It was also a time when Jim Thompson learned, like those who have harboured dreams before, that not everyone was as passionate and committed to the cause. Jim Thompson came from the North-east, where football was and indeed is, an intrinsic part of life. Jim Thompson's enthusiasm was found, by many people, to be infectious, and it was easy to believe his promises of football glory for the club. Perhaps this was because those that listened wanted it, but a lot of it was to do with his persuasive manner. Unfortunately, Jim and the writer didn't always get on eye to eye, which is a shame, because as a 'football man', I had and retain a lot of respect for what he has done. He had the foresight, whether for mercenary reasons or otherwise, to realise that progression is a facet of life that must be maintained. In the bad old days, the strong teams in the Football League, showed commendable 'esprit de corps' by continuing to allow their weaker partners in Division Four to remain. However, Jim Thompson realised that this syndrome undermined the League itself, and lowered the standard.

The lifeblood of any football club are the fans. Therefore they should be well looked after, perhaps even pampered, which they certainly were not at Maidstone United. Information on what was happening was too scarce, and supporters had, too often, to rely on rumours. This was obviously not an ideal situation, but one which at times, many felt Jim Thompson and the Club hierarchy, propagated and almost appeared to sit back and watch everyone debating the matter. What Jim Thompson did appreciate was the potential that Maidstone United held. Unfortunately, it involved relying on certain factors such as passion, commitment, enthusiasm and undying devotion to the club. Sadly for the majority of people living in Maidstone, including those who mattered, such as the Council, these were missing.

Jim Thompson and the board of Directors of the club were charged by the F.A. for misconduct concerning Maidstone United and Dartford F.C. The hearing, in early 1994, found Jim Thompson and the board guilty of failing to notify the F.A. of a change in the groundsharing agreement with Dartford (presumably when Jim Thompson acquired shares in the latter), but only Jim Thompson was punished. He was sentenced to a 3 month football ban, and ordered to pay costs of £13,000. The other Directors, although found guilty, were not punished as it was considered that their involvement in the day to day running of Maidstone United was minimal. Jim Thompson was also sentenced to a 9 month suspended ban from football, for other irregularities. Jim Thompson, in character, as ever, ridiculed the decision, and appealed, which resulted in having the fine quashed. It was clear that he had had enough of football and the problems that it had bought him, and although nothing official was ever announced, his involvement in the 're-born' Maidstone Invicta became less and less. In the summer of 1994, it was announced that Jim Thompson was to become the Chairman of the Maidstone chamber of Commerce.

As for Maidstone Invicta, throughout season 1993-94, they were advertised in the Kent Messenger as 'The new Stones', but in all honesty, this was a tag that was disputed by most ex-Maidstone United fans, who ignored them. There were stories that they intended to apply for membership of the Winstonlead Kent League, although this never happened, and it would seem that it never will. They play ironically enough at the London Road training ground, which is adjacent to the old Athletic Ground site, and which was connected with Maidstone United for so long. The training ground has been transformed into a decent enough pitch, with a footpath and rail surrounding it. However, it belongs to the Mormon church, and even if Invicta did acquire ownership, there is certainly no room for the sort of expansion that would be required to build stands etc. Maidstone Invicta then should be seen in a totally separate light from that of Maidstone United, and as a different club in their own right. Whether they ever gain the affection and support of the townspeople is hard to tell, however at the time of writing they remain a local team with big ambitions, in a local League. Should they wish to pursue those ambitions, then their number one priority must be to move to a larger site, and presumably with the backing of substantial corporate sponsorship. Such a move not only needs the sort of money which Maidstone United so dearly wanted, but also the support of a local Council who would appear to have been down this road and have made their feelings more than clear.

As for Maidstone United, they remain a fond memory for many players and fans, who can only dream of what might have been. They, like the writer, must be content to sit and remember the good times.

JCT/SJA250   31 July 1992

MAIDSTONE UNITED FOOTBALL CLUB LTD

On the 28 July the board of directors received a report
that all avenues being pursued to refinance the Club had
failed except a bid from a consortium led by Mr John Waugh.

The directors considered that in the light of the scheduled
EGM on Tuesday 4 August when the company would almost
certainly be forced into liquidation that their first duty
must be to ensure, if possible, that all creditors of the
company were fully reimbursed and that outstanding wages
due to the company's employees be met.

As Mr Waugh's offer was to pay all creditors 100p in the £1
and bring all staff salaries up to date and it was the only
offer available, the directors agreed to accept.

In order to facilitate this takeover Mr J C Thompson, the
majority shareholder of the Club, therefore agreed to
transfer his majority shareholding for a token
consideration to Mr Waugh.

Following this decision the board of directors and Club
Secretary tendered their resignations.

All further information with regard to Mr Waugh's proposals
will be issued by the new majority shareholder and/or the
new board of directors. The new Club Secretary and Chief
Executive is Mr Peter Ratcliffe.

          J C Thompson   R J Gilbert
          G A Pearson   D J A Berry
          M Mercer   D J Twiddy

In effect the end of Maidstone United F.C. -
the official memo that severed Jim Thompson's interest in the club.

CHAPTER 12

MAIDSTONE UNITED FOOTBALL CLUB

HONOURS, STATISTICS & TRIVIA

The following details Maidstone United's honours as known, and includes all distinctions at Amateur, Semi-professional and Professional level. It is as accurate as research allows, although there is some dispute as far as the early years are concerned, as often the club did not issue programmes, especially when they were amateurs, therefore records are occasionally vague. This is also true with regard to the Kent Senior Cup victories. The Club claimed several victorious years that are not mentioned by the Kent County F.A. who run the competition. These factors must therefore by appreciated.

It should be noted that many of the statistics were provided by Alan Brigden, Maidstone United's official Club Historian, who has a wealth of material and personal memories.

(Maidstone United were officially formed in 1897, although the Club were known as Maidstone Invicta from 1891)

Year Formed: 1897

EAST KENT LEAGUE
Champions: 1897/98, 1898/99, 1900/01.
KENT LEAGUE Div 1
Champions: 1898/99, 1921/22, 1922/23.
Runners-up: 1897/98.
KENT LEAGUE Div 2
Champions: 1981/82, 1982/83.
Runners-up: 1980/81.

THAMES AND MEDWAY COMB.
Winners:1905/06,1906/07,1910/11,1912/13, 1920/21, 1921/22.
Runners-up: 1911/12.

KENT VICTORY CUP
Runners-up: 1919/20.

KENT SENIOR SHIELD
Winners: 1921/22.
Runners-up: 1919/20.

CHATHAM CHARITY CUP
Winners: 1921/22.
Runners-up: 1919/20.

KENT SENIOR CUP
Winners: 1906/7, 1908/09, 1912/13, 1913/14, 1919/20, 1921/22, 1922/23: 1965/66, 1975/76, 1978/79, 1981/82, 1987/88, 1989/90.
Finalists: 1898/99, 1900/01, 1919/20, 1920/21,1963/64, 1973/74, 1974/75, 1977/78, 1979/80,1983/84, 1986/87.

KENT AMATEUR CUP
Winners: 1955/56, 1960/61, 1961/62.
Finalists: 1947/48, 1953/54, 1964/65.

CORINTHIAN LEAGUE
Winners: 1955/56.

CORINTHIAN LEAGUE-NEALE CUP
Runners-up (Reserves): 1954/55

CORINTHIAN LEAGUE MEM'L. SHIELD
Winners: 1955/56

ATHENIAN LEAGUE
Runners-up: 1957/58

BROMLEY HOSPITAL CUP
Winners: 1961/62
KENT FLOODLIT CUP
Winners: 1972/73
Runners-up: 1968/69

SOUTHERN LEAGUE DIV 1 (South)
Winners: 1972/73
KENT MESSENGER TROPHY
Winners: 1973/74
Finalists: 1974/75
EASTERN FLOODLIT LEAGUE (South Thames Section)
Winners: 1975/76, 1976/77.
KENT FLOODLIT TROPHY
Winners: 1976/77, 1977/78

ANGLO DUTCH JUBILEE CUP
Winners: 1977/78
KENT AMATEUR LEAGUE
Champions: 1978/79.
KENT AMATEUR LEAGUE CUP
Winners: 1978/79, 1979/80.
KENT YOUTH CUP
Winners: 1978/79, 1980/81.
Finalists: 1981/82, 1985/86.
KENT YOUTH LEAGUE
Runners-up: 1981/82, 1985/86.
KENT YOUTH LEAGUE CUP
Finalists: 1981/82, 1985/86.

BEAUVAIS INTERNATIONAL YOUTH TOURNAMENT
Winners: 1981/82.
ALLIANCE PREMIER LEAGUE
Champions: 1983/84.
Runners-up: 1982/83.
WEST KENT CHALLENGE CUP
Winners: 1979/80.
Finalists: 1982/83.
ESSEX & HERTS BORDER COMBINATION
Champions: 1983/84, 1986/87.
BORDER COMBINATION CUP
Finalists: 1983/84
ESSEX & HERTS BORDER SPORTSMANSHIP SHIELD
Winners: 1986/87
RADIO KENT 6 A SIDE
Winners: 1984/85
F.BUDDEN TROPHY
Winners: 1984/85
BOB LORD TROPHY
Finalists: 1984/85
STUTCHYBURY FUELS CHALLENGE CUP
Winners: 1986/87
B & W CHAMPIONS CUP
Winners 1987/88

GM VAUXHALL CONFERENCE: Champions: 1988/89
GM VAUXHALL CONFERENCE CHAMPIONSHIP SHIELD: Winners: 1989/90

Major leagues in which Maidstone United competed

	P	W	D	L	F	A	Pts
Kent League (1897-05 & 1909-50)	1030	447	163	440	2018	2200	894
South Eastern League (1905-10)	144	51	25	68	238	321	102
Corinthian (1950-57)	186	79	35	72	420	408	158
Athenian (1957-59)	60	34	13	13	117	74	68
Isthmian (1959-71)	424	118	84	222	600	883	236
Southern Div 1 (1971-73)	72	39	22	11	138	66	78
Southern Premier (1973-79)	252	99	85	68	318	258	198
Alliance Premier (1979-84), Gola (1984-86), GMVC (1986-89)	410	179	113	118	685	492	358
TOTALS:	2578	1046	520	1012	4534	4702	2092

RECORD VICTORY (The Club's first ever match)
Friendly Sept 4th 1897 15-0 v Old St Stephens.

RECORD HOME VICTORIES:
12-0 V Chislett C.W. Oct 4th 1952 - Kent Senior Cup.
11-0 V Swancombe Dec 8th 1900 - Kent League.
11-0 V Dartford April 12th 1902 - Kent League.

RECORD AWAY VICTORIES:
7-0 V Ramsgate Sept 2 1922 - Kent League
8-1 V Callenders Athletic Sept 13th 1969 - FA Amateur Cup
7-0 V Swanley Oct 18th 1967 - FA Amateur Cup replay

RECORD HOME DEFEATS:
9-0 v Tottenham Hotspur Reserves - South Eastern League Nov 17 1906
9-0 v Sittingbourne - Kent League Jan 2 1926
9-0 v Sutton Utd - Isthmian League Sep 21 1967.

RECORD AWAY DEFEATS:
12-1 v Northfleet Feb 13th 1932 - Kent League
11-0 v Margate Feb 15th 1936 - Kent League
11-0 v Northfleet Mar 4th 1936 - Kent League
11-0 v Bromley Feb 11th 1950 - Kent Amateur Cup Final

In a Corinthian League Match (at the Athletic ground) on Feb 10th 1951, the Stones lost to Maidenhead Utd 10-3, this was the only match Maidstone conceded double figures at home.

F.A.CUP: First entered - 1898
RECORD HOME WIN: 9-0 v Borstall Heath Sep 25th 1920
RECORD HOME DEFEAT: 6-0 v Bromley Sept 13th 1952
RECORD AWAY DEFEATS: 8-1 v Clapton Nov 3rd 1900
No significant (goals scored) away victories achieved. 3rd round reached in 1981, 1984, 1987* & 1988. *15,952 saw the Stones 3-1 defeat at Watford on Jan 10th 1987, the largest crowd the club ever played before.

F.A.AMATEUR CUP: First entered 1928
RECORD HOME VICTORY: 9-0 V Bexley Sept 28th 1957
RECORD AWAY VICTORY: 8-1 V Callenders Ath Sept 13th 1969 (Prel.round)
                         7-0 v Swanley Oct 1969 2nd Qual round
RECORD HOME DEFEAT: 7-0 v Romford Feb 1st 1936 2nd Round
                         6-0 v Sutton Utd Mar 2nd 1963 2nd Round (replay)
          The 3rd round was reached in 1960-61.

FA TROPHY: First entered 1972
No significant goalscoring. The Final was reached in 1986-87 season.

ALLIANCE/GOLA/GM VAUXHALL CONFERENCE LEAGUE
National non-League competition founded in 1979

RECORD HOME VICTORY: 6-0 v Bath C April 26th 1980
                           6-0 v Trowbridge T Sept 29th 1982
                           6-0 v Scarborough May 7th 1983
                           6-0 v Telford May 5th 1986

RECORD AWAY DEFEAT: 6-0 v Bath Jan 23rd 1982

A 6-3 victory over Kidderminster was achieved on April 8th 1989 (the first away victory where six goals were scored since a Corinthian League victory, 6-4 at Worthing, on January 21st 1956.

RECORD ATTENDANCE (Athletic Ground, London Rd, Maidstone)
10,591 v Charlton Athletic, F.A.Cup 3rd Round replay, 1979.

RECORD ATTENDANCE (Watling Street, Dartford)
5,008 v Cambridge Utd, Div 4 play off, 2nd leg May 16 1990.

RECORD APPEARANCES:
Fred Baker - 405 (160 consecutive appearances between 1953 - 1958).

RECORD GOALSCORER:
Steve Butler - 176

YOUNGEST PLAYER:
David Sadler - Debut for the Club at just over 15 years of age.

FIRST FULL TIME PROFESSIONAL SIGNED (IN THE FOOTBALL LEAGUE):
Mark Gall.

LAST MATCH AT LONDON ROAD, MAIDSTONE.
23rd April 1988. GM Vauxhall Conference League v Stafford Rangers (3-1 victory)
Team: Cawston, Roast, Hill, Pamphlett, Risk, Glover, Donn, Stewart, Gall, Docker, Rogers.
Subs: Butler, Hoyte.

FIRST FOOTBALL LEAGUE MATCH:
19th August 1989 V Peterborough Utd (away). (1-0 defeat)
Team: Beeney, Barton (Stebbing), Cooper, Berry, Golley, Pearce, Lillis, (Charlery), Elsey, Sorrell, Butler, Gall.

FIRST HOME FOOTBALL LEAGUE VICTORY:
26th August 1989 4-1 v Scarborough
Team: Beeney, Elsey, Cooper, Pamphlett, Golley, Berry, Lillis, Galliers, Sorrell, Butler, Butler, Gall (Charlery),
Sub: Barton (not used). Goalscorers: Butler (3), Lillis.

FIRST AWAY FOOTBALL LEAGUE VICTORY:
16th September 1989 3-2 v Grimsby Town
Team: Beeney, Barton, Rumble, Pamphlett, Golley, Pearce, Cooper, Elsey, Sorrell (Stebbing), Butler, Gall (Charlery).
Goalscorers: Gall (2), Butler.

LAST FOOTBALL LEAGUE MATCH:
2nd May 1992 v Doncaster Rovers (Away). Lost 1-0.
Team: Hesford, Hazel, Thompson, Smalley, Breen, Donegal, Lillis, Stebbing, Sandeman, Ellis, Newman. Subs: Oxbrow, Tutton.

MOST LEAGUE POINTS IN ANY SEASON - 84 (GMVC 1988-89)
FEWEST LEAGUE POINTS IN ANY SEASON - 10 (Isthmian League 1967-68)

MOST CONSECUTIVE LEAGUE WINS - 14 (Kent League 1921-22)
MOST CONSECUTIVE LEAGUE MATCHES WITHOUT A DEFEAT- 25 (1921-22)
MOST CONSECUTIVE HOME LEAGUE MATCHES WITHOUT DEFEAT - 27 (19th April 1952 to 25th Sep 25th 1954 - Corinthian League)

MOST CONSECUTIVE LEAGUE AWAY MATCHES WITHOUT A WIN - 24 (17th Mar 17th 1965 to 24th Aug 24th 1970 - Isthmian League)
MOST CONSECUTIVE LEAGUE DEFEATS - 9 (25th Aug to 17th Nov 1934 Kent League)
MOST CONSECUTIVE LEAGUE MATCHES WITHOUT A WIN -18 (10th Feb 10th 1968 to 7th Sep 1968 Isthmian League)

MOST LEAGUE VICTORIES IN ONE SEASON -26 (Kent League 1922-23)
LEAST LEAGUE VICTORIES IN ONE SEASON -1 (Kent League 1921-22)
MOST LEAGUE DEFEATS IN A SEASON - 31 (Isthmian League 1967-68)

MOST LEAGUE GOALS CONCEDED IN A SEASON - 131 (Isthmian League 1967-68)
FEWEST LEAGUE GOALS CONCEDED IN A SEASON - 10 (Kent League 1922-23)

MOST HOME LEAGUE VICTORIES IN A SEASON - 18 (Alliance Prem. League 1982-83)
FEWEST HOME LEAGUE VICTORIES IN A SEASON - 1 (Corinthian League 1951-52)
MOST AWAY VICTORIES IN A SEASON - 13 (GMVC 1988-89)
FEWEST AWAY VICTORIES IN A SEASON) - 0 (Isthmian League 1969-70 & Kent League. 1927-28)

MOST LEAGUE GOALS IN A SEASON- 96 (Kent League 1922-23)
FEWEST LEAGUE GOALS IN A SEASON - 26 (Isthmian League 1967-68)

MOST GOALS IN ONE GAME FOR MAIDSTONE UNITED - 7
T Thompson v Dartford Kent League 12th April 12th 1902)
B Keene v APM Friendly 20th April 20th 1946)

- *TRIVIA* -

Kenny Hill who played for the club during the 1980's, also worked as a male model.

Stuart Nethercott played for the Stones (on loan from Spurs), moved on to Barnet on loan, and played against Maidstone United in his first match for the Underhill club!

One of the animals on the Stone's badge, although looking like a kangaroo is in fact an iguanadon! The Club badge is based on the town badge, and one of the creatures was found near Maidstone, and thus adopted for the badge.

Stone's long serving supremo, Jim Thompson, was a goalkeeper of some repute for a team based in Liverpool, and in his entry in *"Debrett's People Of Today"*, his hobbies are listed as 'Walking and Northumberland history".

Until the arrival of Steve Butler, the top scorer for Maidstone United was Mickey Angel, who scored 129 in two spells for the club between 1965 and 1974.

In the matchday programme for the last match ever played at the Athletic ground, famous former player, David Sadler wrote: *"I can clearly recall how excited I would get when, as a young boy of 10 or 11, I would be taken to watch the "Stones", and would dream of the chance to play on the ground that I knew as my own Wembley".*

Maidstone United won an award on BBC Radio 1's football club song contest for the 1971-72 season, hosted by Emperor Roscoe, with the Stone's song;

> *Eleven good men in a football team*
> *Make a team of great renown,*
> *Black and gold are the colours they wear*
> *and they play for Maidstone Town,*
> *Maidstone have the cream*
> *in Kent's best football team.*
> *CHORUS*
> *Stones, Stones come on the Stones,*
> *Maidstone can beat 'em today,*
> *Stones, Stones let's have you Stones,*
> *Whether it's home or away,*
> *Let's have goals, bags of lovely goals,*
> *Don't let the other lot win,*
> *So Maidstone United -*
> *Let's bang another one in!*

GM VAUXHALL CONFERENCE 1988-89

Date	Opponents	Att.	Score	Goalscorers	1	2	3	4	5	6	7	8	9	10	11	12	14
Aug 20	Cheltenham T.	1321	4-0	Golley, Gall(3)	Beeney	Berry	Hill	Roast	Beattie	Goyette	Golley	Stewart	Ashford	Gall	Rogers	Jacques	Docker
23	Wycombe Wand.	1674	3-2	Beattie, Stewart, Gall	Beeney	Berry	Hill	Roast	Beattie	Goyette	Golley	Stewart	Ashford	Gall	Sorrell	Jacques	Docker
27	ALTRINCHAM	624	7-2	Hill,Docker,Butler(3),Gall(2)	Beeney	Berry	Docker	Roast	Beattie	Sorrell	Golley	Stewart	Ashford	Butler	Gall	Docker	Rogers
29	RUNCORN	1005	2-2	Butler, Gall	Beeney	Berry	Docker	Roast	Beattie	Sorrell	Golley	Stewart	Ashford	Butler	Gall	Rogers	Jacques
Sep 3	Boston United	2701	4-1	Butler(2), Gall(2)	Beeney	Berry	Docker	Roast	Beattie	Sorrell	Golley	Stewart	Rogers	Butler	Gall	Jacques	Jacques
7	WELLING UNITED	1322	3-0	Stewart, Gall(2)	Beeney	Berry	Docker	Roast	Beattie	Sorrell	Golley	Stewart	Rogers	Butler	Gall	Jacques	Goyette
10	KIDDERMINSTER H.	910	0-3		Beeney	Berry	Hill	Roast	Beattie	Sorrell	Docker	Stewart	Golley	Butler	Gall	Rogers	Goyette
13	Enfield	815	1-1	Gall	Beeney	Berry	Hill	Roast	Beattie	Sorrell	Golley	Golley	Docker	Butler	Gall	Rogers	Jacques
17	Macclesfield Town	1342	3-4	Sorrell, Butler, Gall	Beeney	Berry	Hill	Roast	Beattie	Sorrell	Golley	Stewart	Docker	Butler	Gall	Jacques	Jacques
24	TELFORD UNITED	548	1-3	Butler	Beeney	Berry	Jacques	Pamphlett	Roast	Sorrell	Golley	Roast	Ashford	Butler	Gall	Rogers	Rogers
28	AYLESBURY UTD.	559	1-1	Butler	Beeney	Berry	Hill	Pamphlett	Roast	Collins	Golley	Docker	Ashford	Butler	Gall	Rogers	Collins
Oct 8	Northwich Vic.	700	0-2		Beeney	Berry	Hill	Pamphlett	Roast	Collins	Golley	Stewart	Ashford	Butler	Rogers	Sorrell	Gall
15	CHORLEY	506	2-0	Stewart, Ashford	Beeney	Berry	Hill	Pamphlett	Roast	Collins	Golley	Stewart	Ashford	Butler	Gall	Rogers	Goyette
22	YEOVIL TOWN	638	5-0	Butler(2), Gall(3)	Beeney	Berry	Hill	Pamphlett	Jacques	Collins	Golley	Stewart	Sorrell	Butler	Gall	Goyette	Docker
Nov 5	Kettering Town	2010	3-3	Gall(3)	Beeney	Berry	Hill	Pamphlett	Roast	Collins	Golley	Stewart	Sorrell	Butler	Gall	Rogers	Scotting
12	STAFFORD RANG.	636	3-0	Sorrell, Golley, Gall	Beeney	Berry	Hill	Pamphlett	Roast	Collins	Golley	Goyette	Sorrell	Butler	Gall	Rogers	Beattie
26	Chorley	607	3-1	Roast, Butler(2)	Beeney	Berry	Hill	Pamphlett	Roast	Collins	Golley	Stewart	Jacques	Butler	Gall	Rogers	Jacques
Dec 3	BARNET	1110	3-2	Gall(2), Rogers	Beeney	Berry	Hill	Pamphlett	Roast	Jacques	Golley	Stewart	Sorrell	Butler	Gall	Rogers	Goyette
17	Altrincham	1017	1-0	Gall	Beeney	Berry	Hill	Pamphlett	Roast	Jacques	Golley	Stewart	Sorrell	Butler	Gall	Rogers	Goyette
26	SUTTON UNITED	1063	1-1	Hill	Beeney	Berry	Hill	Pamphlett	Roast	Jacques	Golley	Rogers	Sorrell	Butler	Gall	Scotting	Goyette
31	WYCOMBE WAND.	1127	1-3	Rogers	Beeney	Berry	Scotting	Pamphlett	Roast	Jacques	Golley	Rogers	Sorrell	Butler	Scotting	Goyette	Gall
Jan 2	Sutton United	1179	1-1	Jacques	Beeney	Berry	Scotting	Jacques	Beattie	Collins	Golley	Ashford	Ashford	Butler	Gall	Rogers	Hill
7	Telford United	1146	2-1	Gall, Butler	Beeney	Berry	Scotting	Pamphlett	Roast	Collins	Golley	Sorrell	Ashford	Butler	Gall	Gall	Jacques
21	MACCLESFIELD T.	768	3-3	Berry	Beeney	Berry	Hill	Pamphlett	Collins	Jacques	Golley	Docker	Jacques	Butler	Rogers	Gall	Hill
28	Aylesbury Utd.	1202	2-1	Ashford, Pamphlett	Beeney	Berry	Hill	Pamphlett	Roast	Beattie	Golley	Jacques	Ashford	Butler	Rogers	Gall	Roast
Feb 18	Fisher Athletic	743	2-0	Butler, Pamphlett	Beeney	Berry	Hill	Pamphlett	Roast	Beattie	Golley	Jacques	Ashford	Butler	Rogers	Rogers	Goyette
Mar 1	FISHER ATHLETIC	638	1-0	Butler	Beeney	Berry	Hill	Pamphlett	Roast	Beattie	Golley	Jacques	Ashford	Butler	Gall	Rogers	Collins
4	CHELTENHAM T.	842	2-0	Stewart	Beeney	Berry	Hill	Pamphlett	Roast	Beattie	Stewart	Jacques	Mehmet	Butler	Gall	Charlery	Rogers
11	Yeovil Town	2235	2-1	Mehmet, Golley	Beeney	Berry	Stewart	Pamphlett	Roast	Beattie	Golley	Jacques	Ashford	Butler	Charlery	Gall	Roast
18	KETTERING TOWN	2861	0-0		Beeney	Berry	Hill	Pamphlett	Jacques	Cooper	Golley	Ashford	Ashford	Butler	Charlery	Gall	Roast
25	ENFIELD	1341	3-1	Charlery, Golley, Ashford	Beeney	Berry	Hill	Pamphlett	Jacques	Cooper	Golley	Mehmet	Mehmet	Butler	Charlery	Gall	Roast
27	Welling United	2541	0-0		Beeney	Berry	Hill	Pamphlett	Jacques	Beattie	Golley	Mehmet	Ashford	Butler	Ashford	Gall	Roast
Apr 1	BOSTON UNITED	1033	3-0	Butler(2),Charlery	Beeney	Berry	Hill	Pamphlett	Jacques	Beattie	Golley	Mehmet	Charlery	Butler	Ashford	Roast	Roast
8	Kidderminster H.	1749	6-3	Roast,Gol'y,But'r(3),Pamph't	Beeney	Berry	Hill	Pamphlett	Jacques	Beattie	Golley	Mehmet	Charlery	Butler	Ashford	Gall	Gall
11	Weymouth	956	3-1	Hill, Charlery, Butler	Beeney	Berry	Hill	Pamphlett	Jacques	Beattie	Golley	Mehmet	Charlery	Butler	Ashford	Roast	Roast
22	Stafford Rangers	1253	2-0	Ashford, Charlery	Beeney	Berry	Hill	Pamphlett	Jacques	Beattie	Golley	Mehmet	Charlery	Butler	Ashford	Roast	Gall
26	NORTHWICH VIC.	1345	4-1	Charlery, Butler(2), Golley	Beeney	Berry	Hill	Pamphlett	Jacques	Beattie	Golley	Mehmet	Charlery	Butler	Ashford	Sorrell	Gall
29	WEYMOUTH	1851	3-0	Gall(2), Butler	Beeney	Berry	Hill	Pamphlett	Jacques	Beattie	Golley	Stewart	Gall	Butler	Ashford	Sorrell	Roast
May 3	Barnet	2650	1-2	Gall	Beeney	Berry	Hill	Pamphlett	Jacques	Beattie	Golley	Mehmet	Charlery	Gall	Ashford	Gall	Roast
6	Runcorn	1097	1-0	Gall	Beeney	Berry	Hill	Pamphlett	Jacques	Beattie	Golley	Stewart	Gall	Butler	Ashford	Charlery	Roast
F.A. CUP																	
Nov 19	Newport County	2148	2-1	Hill, Gall	Beeney	Berry	Hill	Pamphlett	Roast	Goyette	Golley	Stewart	Sorrell	Butler	Gall	Rogers	Jacques
Dec 10	Reading	5249	1-1	Sorrell	Beeney	Berry	Hill	Pamphlett	Roast	Jacques	Golley	Stewart	Sorrell	Butler	Gall	Rogers	Collins
14	READING (Replay)	2821	1-2	Gall	Beeney	Berry	Hill	Pamphlett	Roast	Jacques	Golley	Stewart	Sorrell	Butler	Gall	Rogers	Collins
F.A.TROPHY																	
Jan 14	Kidderminster H.	1313	1-2	Ashford	Beeney	Berry	Scotting	Pamphlett	Roast	Collins	Golley	Jacques	Ashford	Butler	Gall	Rogers	Hill
KENT SENIOR CUP																	
Jan 25	DOVER ATH	373	2-2	Rogers(2)	Beeney	Berry	Hill	Pamphlett	Roast	Collins	Golley	Jacques	Sorrell	Butler	Rogers	Gall	Scotting
31	Dover Ath(replay)	1032	3-1	Butler(3)	Beeney	Berry	Scotting	Pamphlett	Roast	Collins	Golley	Jacques	Hill	Butler	Rogers	Gall	Beattie
Mar 14	Dartford	1079	0-0		Beeney	Berry	Stewart	Pamphlett	Roast	Beattie	Golley	Jacques	Gall	Butler	Rogers	Charlery	Sorrell
22	Dartford(replay)	1177	0-0	(3-2 on penalties)	Beeney	Berry	Hill	Pamphlett	Roast	Beattie	Stewart	Jacques	Ashford	Gall	Rogers	Butler	Golley
May 1	Welling Utd *	1744	1-0	Butler (aet)	Beeney	Berry	Hill	Pamphlett	Roast	Beattie	Golley	Jacques	Ashford	Gall	Rogers	Butler	Sorrell

* Final-played at Preistfield Stadium, Gillingham

FOOTBALL LEAGUE DIVISION 4   1989-90

Date		Opponents	Score	Att.	Goalscorers	1	2	3	4	5	6	7	8	9	10	11	12	14
Aug	19	Peterborough Utd	0-1	6522		Beeney	Barton	Cooper	Berry	Golley	Pearce	Lillis	Elsey	Sorrell	Butler	Gall	Charley	Stebbing
	26	SCARBOROUGH	4-1	3372	Butler(3), Lillis	Beeney	Elsey	Cooper	Pamphlett	Golley	Berry	Lillis	Galliers	Sorrell	Butler	Gall	Barton	Charlery
Sep	2	Hereford Utd	0-3	2627		Beeney	Elsey	Cooper	Pamphlett	Golley	Berry	Lillis	Galliers	Sorrell	Butler	Charlery	Pearce	Gall
	9	STOCKPORT COUNTY	0-1	2020		Beeney	Elsey	Cooper	Pamphlett	Golley	Pearce	Charlery	Galliers	Sorrell	Butler	Gall	Barton	Stebbing
	16	Grimsby T	3-2	5198	Gall(2), Butler	Beeney	Barton	Rumble	Pamphlett	Golley	Pearce	Cooper	Elsey	Sorrell	Butler	Gall	Charlery	Stebbing
	23	CHESTERFIELD	0-1	2147		Beeney	Barton	Rumble	Pamphlett	Golley	Pearce	Cooper	Elsey	Sorrell	Butler	Gall	Charlery	Stebbing
	26	Colchester Utd	1-4	2946	Cooper - Pen	Beeney	Barton	Rumble	Pamphlett	Golley	Pearce	Cooper	Elsey	Sorrell	Butler	Charlery	Stebbing	Lillis
	30	CAMBRIDGE UTD	2-2	1706	Smith (og),Lillis	Beeney	Barton	Cooper	Pamphlett	Golley	Pearce	Lillis	Elsey	Sorrell	Butler	Charlery	Stebbing	Gall
Oct	7	BURNLEY	1-2	3762	Cooper	Beeney	Barton	Cooper	Oxbrow	Golley	Pearce	Lillis	Elsey	Charlery	Stebbing	Gall	Sorrell	Roast
	14	Scunthorpe Utd	0-1	3165		Johns	Roast	Rumble	Berry	Oxbrow	Pearce	Lillis	Elsey	Golley	Butler	Barton	Gall	Stebbing
	18	LINCOLN CITY	2-0	2199	Elsey, Lillis	Johns	Barton	Rumble	Berry	Oxbrow	Pearce	Lillis	Elsey	Golley	Butler	Pritchard	Gall	Roast
	21	Southend Utd	1-0	4016	Butler	Beeney	Barton	Rumble	Berry	Oxbrow	Pearce	Lillis	Elsey	Golley	Butler	Pritchard	Gall	Roast
	28	WREXHAM	2-0	1768	Butler, Elsey	Beeney	Barton	Rumble	Berry	Oxbrow	Pearce	Lillis	Elsey	Golley	Butler	Pritchard	Gall	Galliers
	31	Doncaster Rovers	1-1	1806	Golley	Beeney	Barton	Rumble	Berry	Oxbrow	Pearce	Lillis	Elsey	Golley	Butler	Pritchard	Gall	Galliers
Nov	4	Carlisle Utd	2-3	3395	Gall(2)	Beeney	Barton	Rumble	Berry	Oxbrow	Pearce	Lillis	Elsey	Golley	Butler	Pritchard	Charlery	Cooper
	11	YORK CITY	1-0	2043	Butler	Beeney	Barton	Rumble	Berry	Oxbrow	Pearce	Lillis	Elsey	Golley	Butler	Pritchard	Charlery	Cooper
	25	Halifax Town	2-1	1363	Gall, Golley	Beeney	Roast	Cooper	Berry	Oxbrow	Pearce	Gall	Galliers	Golley	Butler	Barton	Charlery	Rumble
Dec	2	EXETER CITY	1-0	1650	Gall	Beeney	Barton	Cooper	Berry	Golley	Pearce	Gall	Elsey	Galliers	Butler	Charlery	Oxbrow	Rumble
	16	HARTLEPOOL UTD	4-2	1501	Rumble,Cooper,Gall(2)	Beeney	Barton	Rumble	Berry	Oxbrow	Golley	Gall	Elsey	Pritchard	Butler	Sorrell	Rumble	Stebbing
	26	Gillingham	2-1	10412	Gall, Butler	Beeney	Barton	Cooper	Berry	Oxbrow	Pearce	Gall	Elsey	Pritchard	Butler	Sorrell	Rumble	Stebbing
	30	Torquay Utd	1-2	2344	Gall	Beeney	Barton	Cooper	Berry	Golley	Pearce	Gall	Elsey	Pritchard	Butler	Sorrell	Charlery	Rumble
Jan	1	ALDERSHOT	5-1	2206	Els'y,Gall,Prith'd(2),Coop'	Beeney	Barton	Cooper	Berry	Oxbrow	Golley	Gall	Elsey	Pritchard	Butler	Sorrell	Rumble	Charlery
	13	Scarborough	1-0	1961	Butler	Beeney	Bartoon	Cooper	Berry	Oxbrow	Golley	Gall	Elsey	Pritchard	Butler	Stebbing	Rumble	Charlery
	20	PETERBOROUGH UTD	1-1	2707	Butler	Beeney	Barton	Cooper	Berry	Oxbrow	Golley	Gall	Elsey	Pritchard	Butler	Sorrell	Lillis	Charlery
	27	Stockport Co	2-1	4161	Butler(2)	Beeney	Barton	Cooper	Berry	Oxbrow	Golley	Gall	Elsey	Pritchard	Butler	Sorrell	Pearce	Lillis
Feb	3	Chesterfield	1-3	4068	Butler	Beeney	Barton	Cooper	Berry	Golley	Pearce	Gall	Elsey	Pritchard	Butler	Sorrell	Oxbrow	Lillis
	10	GRIMSBY TOWN	2-2	2365	Gall, Elsey	Beeney	Barton	Cooper	Berry	Oxbrow	Golley	Gall	Elsey	Pritchard	Butler	Sorrell	Lillis	Charlery
	14	HEREFORD UNITED	2-0	1516	Butler, Gall	Beeney	Barton	Cooper	Berry	Oxbrow	Golley	Gall	Elsey	Pritchard	Butler	Sorrell	Lillis	Roast
	17	Exeter City	0-2	4181		Beeney	Barton	Cooper	Berry	Oxbrow	Golley	Gall	Elsey	Pritchard	Butler	Sorrell	Rumble	Charlery
	24	HALIFAX TOWN	1-2	2182	Golley	Beeney	Roast	Cooper	Berry	Oxbrow	Golley	Gall	Lillis	Pritchard	Butler	Rumble	Sorrell	Stebbing
Mar	3	Rochdale	2-3	2085	Charlery, Sorrell	Beeney	Roast	Cooper	Berry	Oxbrow	Golley	Gall	Elsey	Sorrell	Butler	Pearce	Rumble	Roast
	6	Cambridge Utd	0-2	4464		Beeney	Barton	Cooper	Berry	Golley	Pearce	Gall	Elsey	Pearce	Butler	Sorrell	Lillis	Charlery
	10	COLCHESTER UTD	4-2	2856	Lillis(3), Butler	Beeney	Barton	Cooper	Galliers	Oxbrow	Golley	Gall	Elsey	Sorrell	Butler	Charlery	Lillis	Cooper
	17	Burnley	1-1	5059	Gall	Beeney	Barton	Rumble	Galliers	Rumble	Golley	Gall	Elsey	Sorrell	Rumble	Charlery	Oxbrow	Oxbrow
	21	SCUNTHORPE UTD	1-1	1299	Gall	Johns	Barton	Cooper	Roast	Oxbrow	Golley	Lillis	Elsey	Lillis	Butler	Charlery	Pearce	Roast
	25	Lincoln City	2-1	4302	Lillis(2)	Johns	Barton	Rumble	Berry	Golley	Golley	Gall	Elsey	Lillis	Butler	Charlery	Rumble	Roast
	31	SOUTHEND UTD	3-0	3550	Brush'log),Butler,Lillis	Johns	Barton	Rumble	Berry	Golley	Roast	Gall	Elsey	Lillis	Butler	Charlery	Berry	Pritchard
Apr	4	ROCHDALE	2-0	1501	Rumble, Lillis	Johns	Barton	Rumble	Berry	Golley	Roast	Gall	Elsey	Charlery	Butler	Lillis	Pritchard	Pearce
	7	Wrexham	2-4	2806	Butler(2)	Johns	Barton	Rumble	Berry	Golley	Roast	Gall	Elsey	Charlery	Butler	Lillis	Pritchard	Cooper
	11	DONCASTER ROVERS	1-0	1375	Butler	Johns	Barton	Rumble	Berry	Oxbrow	Roast	Gall	Elsey	Charlery	Butler	Lillis	Pritchard	Oxbrow
	14	Aldershot	2-0	2334	Lillis, Sorrell	Johns	Barton	Pearce	Berry	Golley	Roast	Gall	Elsey	Charlery	Butler	Lillis	Sorrell	Pearce
	16	GILLINGHAM	0-1	5003		Johns	Barton	Pearce	Berry	Golley	Roast	Pritchard	Elsey	Charlery	Butler	Lillis	Sorrell	Sorrell
	21	Hartlepool Utd	2-4	2290	Gall, Butler	Johns	Barton	Cooper	Berry	Golley	Roast	Gall	Elsey	Charlery	Butler	Lillis	Sorrell	Pritchard
	25	TORQUAY UTD	5-1	2223	Lillis(2),Butler,Prit'd	Beeney	Barton	Cooper	Berry	Golley	Roast	Pritchard	Elsey	Charlery	Butler	Lillis	Galliers	Sorrell
	28	York City	0-0	2363		Beeney	Barton	Cooper	Berry	Golley	Roast	Pritchard	Elsey	Oxbrow	Butler	Lillis	Charlery	Sorrell
May	5	CARLISLE UTD	5-2	5006	Gall(2),Lil's,Char'y,Sor'l	Johns	Barton	Cooper	Berry	Golley	Roast	Gall	Elsey	Charlery	Butler	Lillis	Sorrell	Oxbrow

LEAGUE DIVISION 4 - PLAY OFFS

Date		Opponents	Score	Att.	Goalscorers	1	2	3	4	5	6	7	8	9	10	11	12	14
May	13	Cambridge Utd	1-1	7264	Gall	Johns	Barton	Cooper	Berry	Golley	Roast	Gall	Elsey	Charlery	Butler	Lillis	Sorrell	Oxbrow
	16	CAMBRIDGE UTD	0-2	5538	(After extra time)	Johns	Barton	Cooper	Berry	Golley	Roast	Gall	Elsey	Charlery	Butler	Lillis	Sorrell	Oxbrow

(1989/90 Other Competitions)

Date	Opponents	Score	Att.	Goalscorers	1	2	3	4	5	6	7	8	9	10	11	12	14
	F.A.CUP																
Nov 19	YEOVIL TOWN (Rd.1)	2-1	2625	Gall, Barton	Beeney	Barton	Rumble	Berry	Oxbrow	Pearce	Gall	Elsey	Golley	Butler	Pritchard	Cooper	Charlery
Dec 9	EXETER CITY (Rd.2)	1-1	2358	Elsey	Beeney	Barton	Cooper	Berry	Oxbrow	Pearce	Gall	Elsey	Galliers	Butler	Golley	Sorrell	Charlery
13	Exeter C (Rd.2/Rep)	2-3	4125	Butler, Gall	Beeney	Barton	Cooper	Berry	Golley	Pearce	Gall	Elsey	Galliers	Butler	Sorrell	Rumble	Charlery
	LEAGUE CUP																
Aug 22	Cambridge U (Rd1)	1-3	2405	Butler	Beeney	Elsey	Cooper	Pamphlett	Golley	Berry	Lillis	Galliers	Sorrell	Butler	Gall	Barton	Charlery
30	CAMBRIDGE U Rd1/Rep)	0-1	2780		Beeney	Elsey	Cooper	Pamphlett	Golley	Berry	Lillis	Galliers	Sorrell	Butler	Gall	Barton	Charlery
	LEYLAND DAF CUP																
Nov 28	Northampton T (Prel.)	4-2	1663	Gall(3),Golley	Beeney	Roast	Cooper	Berry	Golley	Pearce	Gall	Elsey	Galliers	Butler	Barton	Charlery	Rumble
Jan 10	COLCHESTER U (Prel.)	2-1	1216	Gall, Butler	Beeney	Barton	Cooper	Berry	Golley	Oxbrow	Gall	Elsey	Pritchard	Butler	Sorrell	Rumble	Charlery
17-1-90	MANSFIELD T (Rd.1)	2-1	1020	Butler, Gall	Beeney	Barton	Cooper	Berry	Golley	Oxbrow	Gall	Elsey	Pritchard	Butler	Stebbing	Lillis	Charlery
Feb 21	EXETER C (¼ Fin.South)	2-0	1685	Butler, Gall	Beeney	Barton	Cooper	Berry	Oxbrow	Golley	Gall	Elsey	Roast	Butler	Lillis	Sorrell	Charlery
Mar 14	NOTTS C. (½ Fin.South)	0-1	2158		Johns	Barton	Cooper	Berry	Rumble	Golley	Lillis	Elsey	Charlery	Butler	Sorrell	Oxbrow	Gall
	GM VAUXHALL CONFERENCE CHALLENGE SHIELD																
Oct 4	TELFORD UTD	2-0	464	O.G., Lillis	Beeney	Roast	Rumble	Oxbrow	Golley	Pearce	Lillis	Elsey	Charlery	Stebbing	Kimble	Sorrell	Gall
	FACIT KENT SENIOR CUP																
Jan 24	Canterbury City	3-0	1270	Lillis(2), Roast	Beeney	Roast	Rumble	Pamphlett	Pearce	Oxbrow	Charlery	Elsey	Lillis	Brewer	Cooper	Barton	Butler
Mar 27	Dover Ath (½ Final)	4-2	1400	(After penalties)	Weaver	Roast	Pearce	Galliers	Oxbrow	Golley	Gall	Sorrell	Pritchard	Butler	Lillis	Rumble	Berry
May 7	Gillingham (Final)	1-0	3159	Lillis	Beeney	Roast	Rumble	Galliers	Oxbrow	Pearce	Gall	Brewer	Charlery	Sorrell	Lillis	Toms	Barton

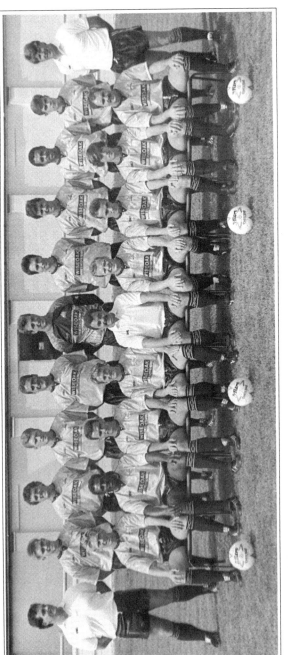

1989/90 Squad

(Back): Steggles (Physio), Lillis, Roast, Butler, Pamphlett, Beeney, Berry, Golley, Charlery, Rumble, Taylor (Assist.Man.)

(Front): Barton, Gall, Pearce, Galliers, Peacock (Manager), Cooper, Kimble, Sorrell, Elsey

FOOTBALL LEAGUE DIVISION 4   1990/91

Date	Opponents	Score	Att.	Goalscorers	1	2	3	4	5	6	7	8	9	10	11	12	14
Aug 25	York City	1-0	2357	Butler	Johns	Roast	Rumble	Berry	Golley	Madden	Charley	Elsey	Pritchard	Butler	Lillis	Sorrell	Gall
Sep 1	NORTHAMPTON T	1-3	2049	Pritchard	Johns	Roast	Rumble	Berry	Golley	Madden	Charley	Elsey	Pritchard	Butler	Lillis	Sorrell	Gall
Sep 8	Carlisle Utd	0-1	3808		Beeney	Roast	Rumble	Berry	Golley	Madden	Pritchard	Osbourne	Charley	Butler	Sorrell	Lillis	Cooper
Sep 15	SCUNTHORPE UTD	6-1	1778	Rumb', Charl'(2) But'(2),Sorr'	Beeney	Roast	Rumble	Berry	Golley	Madden	Pritchard	Osbourne	Charley	Butler	Sorrell	Lillis	Henry
Sep 22	Gillingham	2-0	8004	Pritchard, Osbourne	Beeney	Roast	Rumble	Berry	Golley	Madden	Pritchard	Osbourne	Charley	Butler	Sorrell	Lillis	Cooper
Sep 29	LINCOLN CITY	4-1	2190	Charley(3), Sorrell	Beeney	Roast	Rumble	Berry	Golley	Madden	Lillis	Osbourne	Charley	Butler	Sorrell	Henry	Cooper
Oct 1	Stockport Co	0-1	3207		Johns	Roast	Rumble	Berry	Golley	Madden	Lillis	Osbourne	Henry	Butler	Sorrell	Oxbrow	Cooper
Oct 6	Hartlepool Utd	0-1	2069		Beeney	Roast	Rumble	Berry	Golley	Stebbing	Pritchard	Osbourne	Charley	Butler	Sorrell	Lillis	Stebbing
Oct 13	WALSALL	1-3	2329	Osbourne	Beeney	Osbourne	Rumble	Berry	Golley	Stebbing	Pritchard	Osbourne	Charley	Butler	Sorrell	Lillis	Cooper
Oct 20	DARLINGTON	2-3	2007	Gall, Butler	Beeney	Osbourne	Rumble	Berry	Golley	Oxbrow	Gall	Osbourne	Charley	Butler	Sorrell	Henry	Cooper
Oct 23	Burnley	1-2	5567	Butler	Beeney	Oxbrow	Cooper	Berry	Golley	Stebbing	Gall	Stebbing	Charley	Butler	Cooper	Henry	Charley
Oct 27	Scarborough	2-0	1402	Cooper, Osbourne	Beeney	Oxbrow	Cooper	Berry	Golley	Gilbert	Gall	Osbourne	Charley	Butler	Henry	Lillis	Charley
Oct 31	WREXHAM	0-2	1668		Beeney	Berry	Cooper	Gilbert	Golley	Oxbrow	Gall	Osbourne	Charley	Butler	Henry	Charley	Lillis
Nov 3	CARDIFF CITY	3-0	2010	Berry(2), Butler	Johns	Berry	Cooper	Stebbing	Golley	Oxbrow	Gall	Elsey	Osbourne	Butler	Henry	Pritchard	Gall
Nov 10	HEREFORD UTD	1-1	1034	Cooper-pen	Beeney	Berry	Cooper	Stebbing	Golley	Oxbrow	Gall	Elsey	Osbourne	Butler	Henry	Pritchard	Gall
Nov 24	Aldershot	3-4	2146	Osbourne, Butler, Gall	Beeney	Roast	Cooper	Stebbing	Henry	Oxbrow	Gall	Elsey	Osbourne	Butler	Pritchard	Gall	Charley
Dec 1	PETERBOROUGH UTD	2-0	1920	Gall, Butler	Johns	Roast	Henry	Berry	Golley	Madden	Gall	Elsey	Osbourne	Butler	Stebbing	Lillis	Oxbrow
Dec 15	Blackpool	2-2	2341	Gall, Butler	Beeney	Roast	Henry	Berry	Golley	Stebbing	Gall	Elsey	Osbourne	Butler	Cooper	Charley	Lillis
Dec 22	TORQUAY UTD	2-2	2009	Butler(2)	Johns	Roast	Henry	Berry	Golley	Stebbing	Gall	Elsey	Osbourne	Butler	Cooper	Charley	Rumble
Dec 26	Doncaster Rovers	0-2	2717		Johns	Roast	Rumble	Berry	Golley	Oxbrow	Gall	Elsey	Osbourne	Butler	Cooper	Charley	Rumble
Dec 29	Rochdale	2-3	1776	Gall, Charley	Beeney	Roast	Rumble	Berry	Golley	Madden	Gall	Elsey	Osbourne	Charley	Cooper	Gilbert	Stebbing
Jan 1	CHESTERFIELD	1-0	1793	Butler	Johns	Osbourne	Rumble	Berry	Golley	Stebbing	Gall	Elsey	Osbourne	Butler	Cooper	Gilbert	Oxbrow
Jan 12	Northampton T	0-2	3710		Johns	Roast	Osbourne	Berry	Golley	Stebbing	Madden	Elsey	Charley	Butler	Cooper	Oxbrow	Lillis
Jan 19	YORK CITY	5-4	1840	Butler(3), Charley	Beeney	Henry	Bromage	Berry	Golley	Stebbing	Wimbleton	Elsey	Charley	Butler	Cooper	Oxbrow	Lillis
Jan 26	Scunthorpe Utd	2-2	2703	Charley, Butler	Johns	Henry	Bromage	Berry	Golley	Stebbing	Wimbleton	Elsey	Charley	Butler	Cooper	Gall	Osbourne
Feb 23	Hereford Utd	0-4	2390		Johns	Roast	Bromage	Brown	Oxbrow	Sorrell	Sandeman	Kevan	Charley	Butler	Cooper	Stebbing	Osbourne
Feb 27	HALIFAX TOWN	5-1	1020	Gall(3), Cooper, Butler	Johns	Sandeman	Henry	Brown	Oxbrow	Sorrell	Charley	Kevan	Charley	Butler	Cooper	Elsey	Stebbing
Mar 2	Peterborough Utd	0-2	4623		Johns	Sandeman	Henry	Brown	Oxbrow	Sorrell	Charley	Kevan	Charley	Butler	Cooper	Stebbing	Stebbing
Mar 9	BLACKPOOL	1-1	2253	Butler	Johns	Sandeman	Elsey	Golley	Oxbrow	Stebbing	Charley	Sorrell	Charley	Butler	Stebbing	Osbourne	Osbourne
Mar 12	Stockport County	2-3	1412	Charley, Butler	Beeney	Sandeman	Cooper	Golley	Oxbrow	Elsey	Gall	Sorrell	Charley	Butler	Stebbing	Brewer	Kevan
Mar 16	Lincoln City	1-2	2583	Gall	Beeney	Haylock	Osbourne	Elsey	Oxbrow	Golley	Gall	Sorrell	Charley	Butler	Sandeman	Pullan	Osbourne
Mar 20	Walsall	0-0	2485		Beeney	Haylock	Cooper	Elsey	Oxbrow	Golley	Gall	Sorrell	Charley	Butler	Sandeman	Stebbing	Brewer
Mar 23	HARTLEPOOL UTD	1-4	1704	Butler-Pen	Beeney	Haylock	Cooper	Elsey	Oxbrow	Golley	Gall	Sandeman	Charley	Butler	Stebbing	Osbourne	Osbourne
Mar 30	DONCASTER ROVERS	0-1	1512		Johns	Haylock	Rumble	Oxbrow	Davis	Osbourne	Gall	Sorrell	Lillis	Sorrell	Stebbing	Golley	Pullen
Apr 2	Torquay Utd	1-1	2456	Sorrell	Johns	Haylock	Rumble	Davis	Oxbrow	Osbourne	Gall	Sorrell	Lillis	Stebbing	Sandeman	Golley	Pullen
Apr 6	ROCHDALE	0-1	1340		Johns	Halock	Rumble	Davis	Oxbrow	Osbourne	Henry	Sandeman	Lillis	Sorrell	Stebbing	Golley	Henry
Apr 9	Wrexham	2-2	1029	Henry, Stebbing	Johns	Haylock	Rumble	Oxbrow	Davis	Osbourne	Gall	Sandeman	Henry	Sorrell	Stebbing	Elsey	Pullen
Apr 13	Chesterfield	2-1	3040	Sandeman, Henry	Johns	Haylock	Rumble	Oxbrow	Davis	Osbourne	Gall	Sandeman	Henry	Sorrell	Stebbing	Moore	Golley
Apr 16	Halifax Town	2-3	1001	Gall, Moore	Johns	Haylock	Rumble	Oxbrow	Davis	Sandeman	Gall	Osbourne	Henry	Sorrell	Stebbing	Moore	Golley
Apr 20	Darlington	1-1	4150	Sorrell	Johns	Haylock	Rumble	Oxbrow	Golley	Sandeman	Gall	Osbourne	Elsey	Sorrell	Stebbing	Moore	Golley
Apr 24	GILLINGHAM	3-1	2900	Oxbrow,Sorrell,Butler(og)	Johns	Haylock	Rumble	Oxbrow	Davies	Osbourne	Gall	Sandeman	Henry	Sorrell	Stebbing	Moore	Pullen
Apr 27	BURNLEY	1-0	3130	Gall-pen	Johns	Haylock	Rumble	Oxbrow	Davies	Osbourne	Gall	Sandeman	Henry	Sorrell	Stebbing	Moore	Elsey
May 1	CARLISLE UTD	0-0	1111		Johns	Haylock	Rumble	Oxbrow	Davies	Osbourne	Gall	Sandeman	Henry	Sorrell	Stebbing	Moore	Elsey
May 4	SCARBOROUGH	0-1	1277		Johns	Haylock	Rumble	Oxbrow	Davies	Osvbourne	Gall	Sandeman	Henry	Elsey	Stebbing	Moore	Elsey
May 8	ALDERSHOT	1-1	1298	Elsey	Johns	Haylock	Rumble	Oxbrow	Golley	Osbourne	Gall	Sandeman	Henry	Elsey	Stebbing	Golley	Golley
May 11	Cardiff City	0-0	2011		Johns	Pullen	Rumble	Oxbrow	Davis	Golley	Gall	Sandeman	Henry	Elsey	Stebbing		Moore

(1990/91 Other Competitions)

Date	Opponents	Score	Att.	Goalscorers	1	2	3	4	5	6	7	8	9	10	11	12	14
F.A. CUP																	
Nov 17	TORQUAY UTD (Rd.1)	4-1	2303	Osbourne, Butler(2), Gall	Johns	Berry	Cooper	Stebbing	Golley	Oxbrow	Lillis	Elsey	Osbourne	Butler	Pritchard	Henry	Gall
Dec 8	Aldershot (Rd.2)	1-2	3404	Gall	Johns	Roast	Henry	Berry	Golley	Stebbing	Gall	Elsey	Osbourne	Butler	Lillis	Charlery	Oxbrow
RUMBELOWS CUP																	
Aug 29	LEY. ORIENT (Rd.1/1L)	2-2	2225	Butler(2)	Johns	Roast	Rumble	Berry	Golley	Madden	Charlery	Elsey	Pritchard	Butler	Lillis	Sorrell	Gall
Sep 4	Ley. Orient (Rd.1/2L)	1-4	3429	Butler	Beeney	Roast	Cooper	Berry	Golley	Madden	Gall	Elsey	Pritchard	Butler	Rumble	Lillis	Charlery
LEYLAND DAF CUP																	
Nov 27	Gillingham (Prel.)	1-4	3852	Cooper-Pen	Johns	Berry	Cooper	Stebbing	Golley	Oxbrow	Gall	Elsey	Osbourne	Butler	Charlery	Roast	Lillis
Dec 11	BOURNEMOUTH (Prel.)	3-1	1009	Elsey, Butler, Osbourne	Beeney	Roast	Henry	Berry	Golley	Stebbing	Gall	Elsey	Osbourne	Butler	Cooper	Charlery	Lillis
Jan 8	Southend Utd (Rd.1)	0-2	1849		Beeney	Roast	Rumble	Berry	Golley	Stebbing	Charlery	Elsey	Osbourne	Butler	Cooper	Oxbrow	Lillis
KENT SENIOR CUP																	
Jan 30	DARTFORD	3-2	1065	Gall(2), Butler	Beeney	Henry	Bromage	Berry	Golley	Elsey	Wimbleton	Gall	Charlery	Butler	Cooper	Roast	Osbourne
Mar 5	Gravesend	1-2	858	Charlery	Beeney	Sandeman	Henry	Brown	Golley	Oxbrow	Osbourne	Gall	Charelry	Butler	Stebbing	Cooper	Kevan

Back row (left to right): Ken Steggles (Physiotherapist), Jason Lillis, Dave Madden, Les Berry, Mark Beeney, Mark Golley, Darren Oxbrow, Nicky Johns, Jesse Roast, Steve Butler, Ken Charlery, Tommy Taylor (Assistant Manager).
Front: Paul Rumble, Steve Galliers (Youth Team Manager), Gary Cooper, Mark Gall, Lawrence Osbourne, Keith Peacock (Team Manager) Karl Elsey (Captain), Liburd Henry, Tony Sorrell, Gary Stebbing, Howard Pritchard.

FOOTBALL LEAGUE DIVISION 4   1991/92

Date		Opponents	Score	Att.	Goalscorers	1	2	3	4	5	6	7	8	9	10	11	12	14
Aug	17	Chesterfield	0-3	3444		Hesford	Haylock	Rumble	Oxbrow	Davis	Osbourne	Gall	Painter	Henry	Sandeman	Ellis	Lillis	Cuggy
	24	HALIFAX TOWN	0-1	1216		Hesford	Haylock	Thompson	Oxbrow	Davis	Osbourne	Gall	Painter	Donegal	Sandeman	Rumble	Cuggy	Lillis
	31	Aldershot *	0-3	1864		Hesford	Haylock	Thompson	Oxbrow	Davis	Osbourne	Cuggy	Painter	Donegal	Lillis	Ellis	Henry	Smalley
Sep	4	CARDIFF CITY	1-1	1019	Cuggy-pen	Hesford	Smalley	Thompson	Oxbrow	Davis	Osbourne	Cuggy	Painter	Donegal	Lillis	Rumble	Haylock	Gall
	7	Scunthorpe Utd	0-2	2738		Hesford	Haylock	Thompson	Smalley	Nethercott	Osbourne	Henry	Painter	Donegal	Sandeman	Osbourne	Cuggy	Ellis
	14	WALSALL	2-1	1139	Donegal, Osbourne	Hesford	Davies	Thompson	Smalley	Nethercott	Haylock	Henry	Osbourne	Donegal	Stebbing	Stebbing	Gall	Rumble
	17	LINCOLN CITY	0-2	1113		Hesford	Haylock	Thompson	Nethercott	Davies	Smalley	Painter	Gall	Lillis	Henry	Henry	Haylock	Sandeman
	21	Rotherham	3-3	3870	Henry, Gall, Osbourne	Hesford	Oxbrow	Thompson	Smalley	Nethercott	Davies	Henry	Gall	Painter	Osbourne	Stebbing	Haylock	Rumble
	28	YORK CITY	1-0	1037	Nethercott	Hesford	Oxbrow	Thompson	Oxbrow	Nethercott	Davies	Henry	Gall	Painter	Osbourne	Stebbing	Sandeman	Ellis
Oct	5	Mansfield Town	0-2	3217		Hesford	Sandeman	Thompson	Oxbrow	Nethercott	Davies	Henry	Gall	Painter	Osbourne	Stebbing	Sandeman	Cuggy
	12	DONCASTER ROVERS	2-2	1255	Gall, Osbourne	Hesford	Sandeman	Thompson	Haylock	Oxbrow	Nethercott	Ellis	Stebbing	Richards	Osbourne	Stebbing	Henry	Owers
	19	ROCHDALE	1-1	1016	Sandeman	Hesford	Sandeman	Thompson	Haylock	Oxbrow	Nethercott	Gall	Stebbing	Richa'ds	Osbourne	Hebnry	Painter	Owers
Nov	2	HEREFORD UTD	3-2	842	Hesford,Stebb'g,Richards	Hesford	Sandeman	Thompson	Haylock	Oxbrow	Nethercott	Owers	Stebbing	Richa'ds	Osbourne	Henry	Painter	Smalley
	5	Crewe Alexandra	1-1	2476	Richards	Hesford	Sandeman	Thompson	Haylock	Oxbrow	Nethercott	Painter	Stebbing	Richa'ds	Osbourne	Henry	Painter	Owers
	9	Gillingham	1-1	6716	Osbourne	Hesford	Sandeman	Thompson	Haylock	Davies	Nethercott	Painter	Stebbing	Richards	Osbourne	Henry	Smalley	Cuggy
	23	BURNLEY	0-1	2375		Hesford	Sandeman	Thompson	Haylock	Oxbrow	Nethercott	Painter	Stebbing	Lillis	Osbourne	Henry	Cuggy	Smalley
	30	Carlisle Utd	0-3	2146		Hesford	Sandeman	Thompson	Smalley	Davies	Nethercott	Painter	Stebbing	Donegal	Ellis	Henry	Ellis	Smalley
Dec	21	Halifax Town	1-1	1040	Painter	Hesford	Haylock	Thompson	Smalley	Cuggy	Davies	Painter	Stebbing	Sandeman	Ellis	Henry	Donegal	Tutton
	26	CHESTERFIELD	0-1	1325		Hesford	Haylock	Henry	Smalley	Oxbrow	Davis	Painter	Stebbing	Sandeman	Ellis	Donegal	Tutton	Cuggy
	28	ALDERSHOT *	1-2	1502	Sandeman	Hesford	Haylock	Henry	Smalley	Oxbrow	Davis	Painter	Stebbing	Sandeman	Ellis	Donegal	Tutton	Breen
Jan	1	Cardiff City	5-0	8023	Her',Steb',Paint',Sand'n,Smal'	Hesford	Haylock	Thompson	Smalley	Breen	Davies	Painter	Stebbing	Sandeman	Ellis	Henry	Tutton	Cuggy
	4	BLACKPOOL	0-0	1774		Hesford	Haylock	Henry	Smalley	Breen	Oxbrow	Painter	Stebbing	Sandeman	Ellis	Thompson	Tutton	Cuggy
	8	BARNET	1-1	1988	Davies	Hesford	Haylock	Thompson	Smalley	Breen	Oxbrow	Painter	Stebbing	Sandeman	Ellis	Henry	Donegal	Cuggy
	11	Wrexham	0-0	3167		Hesford	Haylock	Thompson	Smalley	Breen	Oxbrow	Painter	Stebbing	Sandeman	Ellis	Henry	Donegal	Cuggy
	18	NORTHAMPTON TOWN	1-1	1364	Henry	Hesford	Haylock	Thompson	Smalley	Breen	Oxbrow	Painter	Stebbing	Sandeman	Ellis	Henry	Donegal	Cuggy
Feb	12	CARLISLE UTD	5-1	944	Lillis,Henry, Sandeman(3)	Hesford	Haylock	Thompson	Smalley	Breen	Oxbrow	Lillis	Stebbing	Sandeman	Ellis	Henry	Painter	Donegal
	15	Barnet	2-3	2871	Davies, Painter	Hesford	Haylock	Thompson	Smalley	Breen	Oxbrow	Lillis	Stebbing	Sandeman	Ellis	Henry	Painter	Donegal
	22	WREXHAM	2-4	3167	Lillis, Stebbing	Hesford	Haylock	Thompson	Smalley	Breen	Oxbrow	Lillis	Stebbing	Sandeman	Ellis	Henry	Cuggy	Donegal
	29	Blackpool	1-1	4301	Lillis	Hesford	Haylock	Thompson	Smalley	Breen	Davies	Lillis	Stebbing	Sandeman	Ellis	Henry	Ellis	Rutter
Mar	3	Northampton Town	0-1	1677		Hesford	Haylock	Thompson	Smalley	Newman	Oxbrow	Painter	Stebbing	Sandeman	Ellis	Henry	Ellis	Donegal
	7	SCARBOROUGH	2-1	1019	Smalley, Painter	Hesford	Haylock	Thompson	Smalley	Breen	Oxbrow	Lillis	Stebbing	Sandeman	Ellis	Newman	Ellis	Donegal
	11	CREWE ALEXANDRA	2-0	1174	Painter, Henry	Hesford	Haylock	Thompson	Smalley	Breen	Oxbrow	Lillis	Stebbing	Sandeman	Ellis	Painter	Ellis	Newman
	14	Hereford Utd	2-2	1910	Haylock, Henry	Hesford	Haylock	Newman	Smalley	Breen	Oxbrow	Lillis	Stebbing	Newman	Ellis	Painter	Ellis	Newman
	21	GILLINGHAM	1-1	3264	Henry	Hesford	Haylock	Hazel	Smalley	Breen	Oxbrow	Lillis	Stebbing	Newman	Ellis	Painter	Cuggy	Cuggy
	28	Burnley	1-2	10986	Newman	Hesford	Haylock	Thompson	Smalley	Breen	Oxbrow	Lillis	Stebbing	Sandeman	Ellis	Painter	Donegal	Newman
	31	Walsall	1-1	2045	Oxbrow	Hesford	Hazel	Thompson	Smalley	Breen	Oxbrow	Lillis	Stebbing	Sandeman	Ellis	Painter	Donegal	Donegal
Apr	4	SCUNTHORPE UTD	0-1	1237		Hesford	Haylock	Thompson	Smalley	Breen	Oxbrow	Lillis	Stebbing	Sandeman	Ellis	Henry	Cuggy	Cuggy
	7	Rochdale	2-1	2248	Sandeman, Lillis	Hesford	Haylock	Thompson	Smalley	Breen	Oxbrow	Lillis	Stebbing	Newman	Ellis	Henry	Cuggy	Cuggy
	11	Lincoln City	0-1	2241		Hesford	Donegal	Thompson	Smalley	Breen	Oxbrow	Lillis	Stebbing	Sandeman	Ellis	Henry	Tutton	Tutton
	18	ROTHERHAM UTD	0-0	1744		Hesford	Hazel	Thompson	Smalley	Oxbrow	Donegal	Lillis	Stebbing	Sandeman	Ellis	Sinclair	Hazel	Hazel
	20	York City	1-1	2241	Sandeman	Hesford	Hazel	Thompson	Smalley	Breen	Newman	Lillis	Stebbing	Sandeman	Ellis	Henry	Tutton	Tutton
	25	MANSFIELD TOWN	0-0	1602		Hesford	Hazel	Thompson	Smalley	Breen	Henry	Lillis	Stebbing	Sandeman	Ellis	Newman	Oxbrow	Oxbrow
	29	Scarborough	0-2	939		Hesford	Hazel	Thompson	Smalley	Oxbrow	Donegal	Lillis	Stebbing	Sandeman	Ellis	Newman	Donegal	Donegal
May	2	Doncaster Rovers	0-3	1680		Hesford	Hazel	Thompson	Smalley	Breen	Donegal	Lillis	Oxbrow	Sandeman	Ellis	Henry	Tutton	Tutton

* Game expunged from record following Aldershot's resignation from the League.

(1991/92 Other Competitions)

Date	Opponents	Score	Att.	Goalscorers	1	2	3	4	5	6	7	8	9	10	11	12	14
F.A.CUP																	
Nov 16	SUTTON UNITED	1-0	2008	Thompson	Hesford	Sandeman	Thompson	Haylock	Oxbrow	Davis	Painter	Stebbing	Cuggy	Osbourne	Henry	Lillis	Smalley
7	KETTERING TOWN	1-2	2750	Henry	Hesford	Sandeman	Thompson	Haylock	Oxbrow	Davis	Smalley	Stebbing	Donegal	Osbourne	Henry	Painter	Lillis
RUMBELOWS CUP																	
Aug 21	Leicester C. (Rd.1/1L)	0-3	9610		Hesford	Haylock	Thompson	Oxbrow	Davis	Osbourne	Gall	Painter	Donegal	Sandeman	Rumble	Lillis	Cuggy
28	LEICESTER C. (Rd.1/2L)	0-1	1638		Hesford	Haylock	Thompson	Oxbrow	Davis	Osbourne	Cuggy	Painter	Donegal	Lillis	Ellis	Gall	Smalley
AUTOGLASS TROPHY																	
Nov 23	FULHAM (Prel.)	2-6	937	Gall, Owers	Hesford	Sandeman	Thompson	Haylock	Oxbrow	Nethercott	Gall	Stebbing	Richards	Osbourne	Henry	Painter	Owers
Dec 10	Gillingham (Prel.)	2-4	2300	Ellis, Osbourne	Hesford	Sandeman	Thompson	Haylock	Davis	Oxbrow	Henry	Stebbing	Ellis	Osbourne	Smalley	Painter	Donegal
KENT SENIOR CUP																	
Oct 2	DARTFORD	1-2	531	Ellis	Hesford	Oxbrow	Thompson	Haylock	Smalley	Davis	Henry	Sandeman	Gall	Osbourne	Stebbing	Cuggy	Ellis

Brendan Ormsby, the Doncaster Rovers captain, scores from the penalty spot; this turned out to be the last ever goal scored against the Stones. (2nd May 1992)

(Photo: Paul Gilligan)